W9-BTC-978

Also by the Editors at America's Test Kitchen

Kitchen Hacks

100 Recipes: The Absolute Best Ways to Make the True Essentials

The New Family Cookbook

The Complete Vegetarian Cookbook

The Complete Cooking for Two Cookbook

The America's Test Kitchen Cooking School Cookbook

The Cook's Illustrated Meat Book

The Cook's Illustrated Baking Book

The Cook's Illustrated Cookbook

The Science of Good Cooking

The America's Test Kitchen Menu Cookbook

The America's Test Kitchen Quick Family Cookbook

The America's Test Kitchen Healthy Family Cookbook

The America's Test Kitchen Family Baking Book

THE AMERICA'S TEST KITCHEN LIBRARY SERIES:

The Best Mexican Recipes

The Make-Ahead Cook

The How Can It Be Gluten-Free Cookbook Volume 2

The How Can It Be Gluten-Free Cookbook

Healthy Slow Cooker Revolution

Slow Cooker Revolution Volume 2: The Easy-Prep Edition

Slow Cooker Revolution

The Six-Ingredient Solution

Comfort Food Makeovers

The America's Test Kitchen D.I.Y. Cookbook

Pasta Revolution

Simple Weeknight Favorites

The Best Simple Recipes

THE COOK'S COUNTRY SERIES:

Cook's Country Eats Local

From Our Grandmothers' Kitchens

Cook's Country Blue Ribbon Desserts

Cook's Country Best Potluck Recipes

Cook's Country Best Lost Suppers

Cook's Country Best Grilling Recipes

The Cook's Country Cookbook

THE TV COMPANION SERIES:

The Complete Cook's Country TV Show Cookbook

The Complete America's Test Kitchen TV Show Cookbook 2001–2016

America's Test Kitchen: The TV Companion Cookbook (2002–2009 and 2011–2015 Editions)

AMERICA'S TEST KITCHEN ANNUALS:

The Best of America's Test Kitchen (2007–2016 Editions)

Cooking for Two (2010–2013 Editions)

Light & Healthy (2010–2012 Editions)

THE BEST RECIPE SERIES:

The New Best Recipe

More Best Recipes

The Best One-Dish Suppers

Soups, Stews & Chilis

The Best Skillet Recipes

The Best Slow & Easy Recipes

The Best Chicken Recipes

The Best International Recipe

The Best Make-Ahead Recipe

The Best 30-Minute Recipe

The Best Light Recipe

The Cook's Illustrated Guide to Grilling and Barbecue

Best American Side Dishes

Cover & Bake

Steaks, Chops, Roasts & Ribs

Baking Illustrated

Italian Classics

American Classics

FOR A FULL LISTING OF ALL OUR BOOKS:

CooksIllustrated.com

AmericasTestKitchen.com

Praise For Other America's Test Kitchen Titles

"There are pasta books . . . and then there's this pasta book. Flip your carbohydrate dreams upside down and strain them through this sieve of revolutionary, creative, and also traditional recipes."
SAN FRANCISCO BOOK REVIEW ON *PASTA REVOLUTION*

"Ideal as a reference for the bookshelf . . . , this volume will be turned to time and again for definitive instruction on just about any food-related matter."
PUBLISHERS WEEKLY ON
THE SCIENCE OF GOOD COOKING

"The perfect kitchen home companion. The practical side of things is very much on display. . . . cook-friendly and kitchen-oriented, illuminating the process of preparing food instead of mystifying it."
THE WALL STREET JOURNAL ON
THE COOK'S ILLUSTRATED COOKBOOK

"If this were the only cookbook you owned, you would cook well, be everyone's favorite host, have a well-run kitchen, and eat happily every day."
THECITYCOOK.COM ON *THE AMERICA'S
TEST KITCHEN MENU COOKBOOK*

"This book upgrades slow cooking for discriminating, 21st-century palates—that is indeed revolutionary."
THE DALLAS MORNING NEWS ON
SLOW COOKER REVOLUTION

"Forget about marketing hype, designer labels, and pretentious entrées: This is an unblinking, unbedazzled guide to the Beardian good-cooking ideal."
THE WALL STREET JOURNAL ON
THE BEST OF AMERICA'S TEST KITCHEN 2009

"Expert bakers and novices scared of baking's requisite exactitude can all learn something from this hefty, all-purpose home baking volume."
PUBLISHERS WEEKLY ON *THE AMERICA'S
TEST KITCHEN FAMILY BAKING BOOK*

"Scrupulously tested regional and heirloom recipes."
THE NEW YORK TIMES ON
THE COOK'S COUNTRY COOKBOOK

"If you're hankering for old-fashioned pleasures, look no further."
PEOPLE MAGAZINE ON *AMERICA'S
BEST LOST RECIPES*

"This tome definitely raises the bar for all-in-one, basic, must-have cookbooks. . . . Kimball and his company have scored another hit."
THE OREGONIAN ON *THE AMERICA'S
TEST KITCHEN FAMILY COOKBOOK*

"A foolproof, go-to resource for everyday cooking."
PUBLISHERS WEEKLY ON *THE AMERICA'S
TEST KITCHEN FAMILY COOKBOOK*

"The strength of the Best Recipe series lies in the sheer thoughtfulness and details of the recipes."
PUBLISHERS WEEKLY ON THE BEST RECIPE SERIES

"These dishes taste as luxurious as their full-fat siblings. Even desserts are terrific."
PUBLISHERS WEEKLY ON *THE BEST LIGHT RECIPE*

"Further proof that practice makes perfect, if not transcendent. . . . If an intermediate cook follows the directions exactly, the results will be better than takeout or Mom's."
THE NEW YORK TIMES ON *THE NEW BEST RECIPE*

"Like a mini–cooking school, the detailed instructions and illustrations ensure that even the most inexperienced cook can follow these recipes with success."
PUBLISHERS WEEKLY ON *BEST AMERICAN
SIDE DISHES*

"Makes one-dish dinners a reality for average cooks, with honest ingredients and detailed make-ahead instructions."
THE NEW YORK TIMES ON *COVER & BAKE*

"The best instructional book on baking this reviewer has seen."
THE LIBRARY JOURNAL (STARRED REVIEW) ON
BAKING ILLUSTRATED

PRESSURE COOKER
COOKER
PERFECTION

100 FOOLPROOF RECIPES THAT WILL
Change the Way You Cook

BY THE EDITORS AT
America's Test Kitchen

PHOTOGRAPHY BY
Keller + Keller and Daniel J. van Ackere

Copyright © 2013
by the Editors at America's Test Kitchen

All rights reserved. No part of this book may
be reproduced or transmitted in any manner
whatsoever without written permission from
the publisher, except in the case of brief quo-
tations embodied in critical articles or reviews.

AMERICA'S TEST KITCHEN
17 Station Street, Brookline, MA 02445

Library of Congress
Cataloging-in-Publication Data
Pressure Cooker Perfection: 100 foolproof
recipes that will change the way you cook
/ by the editors at America's test kitchen ;
photography by Keller + Keller and Daniel
J. van Ackere — 1st ed.
    pages cm
  Includes index.
  ISBN 978-1-936493-41-8
1. Cooking, American. I. America's test
kitchen (Television program) II. Title: Pressure
cooker perfection.

Manufactured in the United States of America
10 9 8 7 6 5

PAPERBACK: US $19.95 / $19.95 CAN

Distributed by Penguin Random House
Publisher Services / tel: 800-733-3000

EDITORIAL DIRECTOR: Jack Bishop

EDITORIAL DIRECTOR, BOOKS: Elizabeth Carduff

EXECUTIVE FOOD EDITOR: Julia Collin Davison

SENIOR EDITOR: Louise Emerick

ASSOCIATE EDITORS: Christie Morrison and Dan Zuccarello

ASSISTANT EDITOR: Alyssa King

TEST COOKS: Danielle DeSiato and Ashley Moore

ASSISTANT TEST COOKS: Stephanie Pixley and Lainey Seyler

DESIGN DIRECTOR: Amy Klee

ART DIRECTOR: Greg Galvan

DESIGNER: Taylor Argenzio

FRONT COVER PHOTOGRAPHY: Daniel J. van Ackere

STAFF PHOTOGRAPHER: Daniel J. van Ackere

ADDITIONAL PHOTOGRAPHY: Keller + Keller and Stephen Klise

FOOD STYLING: Catrine Kelty and Marie Piraino

PHOTOSHOOT KITCHEN TEAM:

    ASSOCIATE EDITOR: Chris O'Connor

    ASSISTANT TEST COOKS: Daniel Cellucci and Sarah Mayer

PRODUCTION DIRECTOR: Guy Rochford

SENIOR PRODUCTION MANAGER: Jessica Quirk

SENIOR PROJECT MANAGER: Alice Carpenter

PRODUCTION AND TRAFFIC COORDINATORS: Brittany Allen and Kate Hux

WORKFLOW AND DIGITAL ASSET MANAGER: Andrew Mannone

PRODUCTION AND IMAGING SPECIALISTS: Judy Blomquist,
Heather Dube, Lauren Pettapiece, and Lauren Robbins

COPYEDITOR: Debra Hudak

PROOFREADER: Ann-Marie Imbornoni

INDEXER: Elizabeth Parson

PICTURED ON FRONT COVER: Classic Pot Roast and Potatoes (page 96), Barbecued Baby
Back Ribs (page 124), Artichokes with Lemon-Garlic Butter (page 136), Macaroni and
Cheese (page 52)

PICTURED ON BACK COVER: Whole Chicken with Rosemary and Lemon Sauce (page 112),
Asian-Style Boneless Beef Short Ribs (page 108)

CONTENTS

Welcome to America's Test Kitchen

This book has been tested, written, and edited by the folks at America's Test Kitchen, a very real 2,500-square-foot kitchen located just outside of Boston. It is the home of *Cook's Illustrated* magazine and *Cook's Country* magazine and is the Monday-through-Friday destination for more than three dozen test cooks, editors, food scientists, tasters, and cookware specialists. Our mission is to test recipes over and over again until we understand how and why they work and until we arrive at the "best" version.

We start the process of testing a recipe with a complete lack of conviction, which means that we accept no claim, no theory, no technique, and no recipe at face value. We simply assemble as many variations as possible, test a half-dozen of the most promising, and taste the results blind. We then construct our own hybrid recipe and continue to test it, varying ingredients, techniques, and cooking times until we reach a consensus. The result, we hope, is the best version of a particular recipe, but we realize that only you can be the final judge of our success (or failure). As we like to say in the test kitchen, "We make the mistakes, so you don't have to."

All of this would not be possible without a belief that good cooking, much like good music, is indeed based on a foundation of objective technique. Some people like spicy foods and others don't, but there is a right way to sauté, there is a best way to cook a pot roast, and there are measurable scientific principles involved in producing perfectly beaten, stable egg whites. This is our ultimate goal: to investigate the fundamental principles of cooking so that you become a better cook. It is as simple as that.

You can watch us work (in our actual test kitchen) by tuning in to *America's Test Kitchen* (AmericasTestKitchenTV.com) or *Cook's Country from America's Test Kitchen* (CooksCountryTV.com) on public television, or by subscribing to *Cook's Illustrated* magazine (CooksIllustrated.com) or *Cook's Country* magazine (CooksCountry.com). We welcome you into our kitchen, where you can stand by our side as we test our way to the "best" recipes in America.

Introduction

Twenty years ago, I bought a copy of Lorna Sass's *Cooking Under Pressure* and spent the next six months making everything from pot roast to, believe it or not, cheesecake. I was a convert, but, like most specialty kitchen tools, my pressure cooker ended up under the counter and, eventually, in the basement.

Since that time, two things have happened. First, pressure cookers have become both much better designed and also more reliable. Second, our test kitchen has spent the last year testing and developing recipes to make this appliance one that you will use, if not every day then at least every week. You can do almost anything in a pressure cooker, from Macaroni and Cheese to Barbecued Baby Back Ribs, and the results are always faster and usually better to boot. And some recipes are so spectacularly quick and delicious (Parmesan Risotto takes only 6 minutes of cooking under pressure) that you will never make them again using traditional methods.

Some of my favorite recipes are Farmhouse Chicken Noodle Soup (20 minutes under pressure), Italian Meatloaf (25 minutes), Sirloin Beef Roast with Mushroom Sauce (20 minutes), and, perhaps my favorite pressure cooker recipe of all time, a fabulous recipe for Chicken Broth that takes just 1 hour. I will use a pressure cooker for that last recipe alone. And, of course, pressure cookers are terrific for speeding up everyday chores such as cooking beans, rice, grains, and tough cuts of meat.

The best thing about the pressure cooker is that there are very few trade-offs for the time savings. Unlike a microwave oven, cooking under pressure actually produces better food, and there is nothing finicky about it—the shape or size of various items makes no difference in cooking time. You can put really good food on the table fast without feeling like you have taken shortcuts on quality.

In the many months of testing, we did come across an interesting fact. Almost all the times listed for basic pressure cooker recipes (vegetables, grains, etc.) were incorrect. We spent weeks testing the basics, getting the timing right, and we have included reliable charts so that you can use the pressure cooker as a useful cooking tool day in and day out. We also tested electric pressure cookers (we prefer stovetop models) since they very often produce different results. Now you can use either type and be guaranteed of success.

This of course reminds me of a story. Many years ago when telephones had party lines (I grew up with such a phone), each customer had their own "ring." It seems that our road commissioner, Sonny, went to visit an old bachelor farmer who lived alone. The year before, the farmer's friends suggested that he install a phone, which was now ringing insistently—one long and three short—as the commissioner walked through the door. Sonny asked, "Ain't that your ring?" The old-timer guessed that it was. The commissioner then asked, "Well, why don't you answer the damn thing?"

"Sonny," came the reply, "I had that phone put in for my convenience!"

That's the problem with so many smart, new kitchen appliances. They are supposed to make your life easier, but so many of them actually make cooking harder since they have limited use or they take a lot of practice to use them well. *Pressure Cooker Perfection* is our attempt to take the mystery out of this incredibly useful kitchen tool, one that offers a two-for-one—faster food but also better food. It's a hard combination to beat.

Now I know that all of this sounds a bit like a late-night infomercial. "It's fast, it's easy, and if you act now we will also send you…" Just as I have adopted the slow cooker as a key part of my repertoire (especially during the summer when I want to spend more time outside), the pressure cooker has now found its way back out of the basement and into my kitchen. In fact, it sits on a burner on the back of my stove all the time, a reminder that I can cook quickly and well simply by cooking under pressure.

CHRISTOPHER KIMBALL
Founder and Editor,
Cook's Illustrated and *Cook's Country*
Host, *America's Test Kitchen* and
Cook's Country from America's Test Kitchen

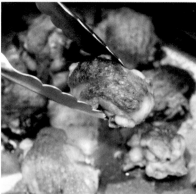

PRESSURE COOKER 101

Why You Should Own a Pressure Cooker

If you're not sure investing in a pressure cooker is worth it, here are several reasons why we are convinced every kitchen should be equipped with one:

1. TODAY'S PRESSURE COOKERS ARE FOOLPROOF: Modern pressure cookers are quieter and far easier to use than the old-fashioned jiggle-top models. They have simple, intuitive methods for locking and unlocking the lid and reading and maintaining pressure levels.

2. THEY'RE SAFE: You've heard the old stories about exploding pressure cookers and meals that ended up on the kitchen ceiling instead of the dinner plates. But that was yesterday. If too much pressure builds up in one of today's pressure cookers, there are multiple safety features that allow that excess pressure to escape safely—and without creating a mess.

3. "FAST FOOD" GETS REDEFINED: Pressure cookers are ideal for the cook who is short on time but doesn't want to be limited to quick recipes, frozen meals, and takeout. A pressure cooker makes braises, stews, and numerous other traditionally long-cooked meals a weeknight option. From-scratch family dinners are back with recipes like our Macaroni and Cheese, Barbecued Baby Back Ribs, and Shredded Pork Soft Tacos. Or cook for a crowd with recipes like Texas-Style Chili con Carne and Turkey Breast and Gravy without losing the day to cooking.

4. PRESSURE COOKERS ARE VERSATILE: Sure, a pressure cooker is ideal for more efficiently cooking big cuts of meat like our Classic Pot Roast and Pulled Pork, soups and stews like Farmhouse Chicken Noodle Soup and Chipotle Pork and Hominy Stew, and pasta sauces like Garden Tomato Sauce and Beef Ragu. But you can also cook beans, grains, and long-cooking vegetables in a fraction of their traditional cooking times. Long-grain brown rice is ready in less than 15 minutes, white rice in a mere 3 minutes. Barbecued beans made with dried beans are ready five times faster than if you were using the oven method, while butternut squash and beets turn fork-tender in 20 minutes or less. You can even make an ultracreamy Parmesan Risotto; all it needs is 6 minutes under pressure, then 6 more of stirring before it's ready for the table.

5. EVERY DISH HAS MORE CONCENTRATED FLAVORS: Pressure cooking translates to maximum concentrated flavor because the volatile flavor molecules can't escape the enclosed environment like they would from a piece of traditional stovetop cookware. Less liquid required and a sealed pot means more flavor stays in the pot—and in the food. For our Pulled Pork, there was no need to let the meat rest for several hours covered in the spice rub to become infused with flavor (a step we require when using the grill or oven) since the pressure cooker made that happen right in the pot. And because of the pressure, the natural juices also stay put. Whole chickens, pork tenderloins, and sirloin beef roast come out ultrajuicy, tender, and cooked to perfection. For all of these reasons, the pressure cooker is also the ultimate piece of cookware for making stocks.

6. PRESSURE COOKERS SAVE YOU MONEY: Pressure cookers cook food in less time than conventional methods, plus you lower the burner level from high to low or medium-low once pressure has been reached. Shorter cooking times and cooking over lower heat translate to less energy used than conventional stovetop recipes. And from a grocery-shopping standpoint, you can also save some money since tough cuts of meat and dried beans, both relatively inexpensive, are ideal for the pressure cooker.

7. PRESSURE COOKERS HELP YOU KEEP A COOLER KITCHEN: For many of the same reasons that make a pressure cooker a money saver, it's also a great summertime appliance. Shorter cooking times, lower burner levels, and heat staying trapped in the pot all keep your kitchen cooler.

How Cooking Under Pressure Works

Pressure cookers function based on a very simple principle: In a tightly sealed pot, the boiling point of liquid is higher.

In a normal cooking vessel, water boils at 212 degrees Fahrenheit. When water boils, it turns to steam, and steam usually stays at 212 degrees. But everything changes in a closed environment. When water is brought to a boil in a pressure cooker, the water molecules can't escape, increasing the pressure within. More energy is needed for the water to boil and steam, which in turn increases the temperature in the chamber. You can raise the pressure inside most pressure cookers to about 15 pounds above normal sea-level pressure, which in turn raises the boiling point of water to 250 degrees.

This means that you are cooking food with steam that's at a temperature up to 38 degrees higher than what's possible in a normal pot. That translates to shorter cooking times, and since cooking requires much less liquid than usual, flavors concentrate. You also use less energy because you turn the heat down just enough to maintain the pressure level within the pot.

THE LANGUAGE OF THE PRESSURE COOKER

High and Low Pressure: Most pots have two pressure levels: high and low. The exact amount of pressure (measured in pounds per square inch, or psi) for each level varies slightly from pot to pot, but generally, high registers around 15 psi, while low pressure registers 5 psi. We use high pressure in most recipes since it is the most efficient, but we found low pressure produces slightly better results when cooking foods that need a more gentle hand, like some grains, rice, and beans. Since not all pressure cookers come with a low setting, we did develop options that rely on high pressure and deliver good results.

Natural and Quick Release: Once the cooking-under-pressure time specified in a recipe is up, you have to let the pressure out of the pot using one of two methods: natural release or quick release.

For a natural release, you turn off the heat and allow the pressure in the pot to naturally drop back down. This is the preferred method when you want to gently finish cooking the food through, since the food will continue to cook as the pressure drops. For instance, large cuts of meat benefit from a natural release by ensuring tender results. If you quickly release the pressure on a large cut of meat like our Sirloin Beef Roast with Mushroom Sauce, the meat will seize up and will have a tough texture come serving time.

A quick release is used when you want to stop the cooking immediately because the food can easily overcook (think chicken breasts). Or, if a gentle finish isn't important, we simply opt for a quick release because it's faster. Modern pressure cookers are equipped with quick-release valves that quickly and safely release the steam from the pot.

Don't try to swap one release method for the other. When using a natural release, the food continues to cook as the pressure comes down. Therefore, if you switch from a natural to a quick release, you are going to undercook the food (and likely also cause problems in terms of final texture of the food). And if you switch from a quick to a natural release, the food will overcook.

Lock the Lid in Place: Before you are able to bring the pot up to pressure, modern pressure cookers have a safety mechanism that requires you "lock the lid in place." The process is a little different on each model. You typically need to line up a marker on the lid with a marker on the pot, then twist the lid so that the handle on the lid aligns with the handle on the pot, thus creating an airtight seal. You may need to flip a locking switch, or make sure a locking indicator signals the pot is properly shut. If the lid is not properly locked on, today's pots are designed so that pressure cannot build up.

The Anatomy of a Pressure Cooker

1 Cooking Pot: The main body of pressure cookers can be made from aluminum or stainless steel. They are made much like a standard-issue pot (which means you can also use it for other occasions when you need a large pot, like cooking pasta and deep frying). Though more expensive, we prefer the stainless pots since they're more durable.

2 Lid: This is no ordinary lid. Pressure-cooker lids are specially designed to create an airtight seal, with the help of the silicone gasket (#10), when properly locked in place on the pot.

3 Disk Base: Typically made from aluminum, the disk base is a key feature because it retains and regulates heat. We found that the thicker the disk base, the more quickly the pot reaches pressure and the more steady and hands-off the cooking is.

4 Primary Handle: Most pots have a long two-piece handle that also contains other components key to the functioning of the pressure cooker, including steam release valves, the pressure regulator (#8), and the pressure indicator (#7). The lid and bottom of the pot both have a handle piece; when the lid is properly locked in place the two parts line up.

5 Secondary Handle: Opposite the primary handle, this grip is a useful secondary support when moving a full, heavy pot.

6 Pressure Safety Lock/Locked Lid Indicator: Some pressure cookers have a button you have to slide into place to lock the pot once the lid has been properly closed; others simply have an indicator (for example, a window that displays red or green) to signify whether the lid is locked. The pot will not trap pressure unless the lid is properly locked in place. We found the locks on some pots were more intuitive to use than others.

7 Pressure Indicator: Every pressure cooker has a way to indicate that pressure has been reached—critical to know since this is when you turn down the heat to maintain the pressure level and start counting the cooking time. The pressure indicator is typically a pin or button that rises as pressure inside the pot increases. If the pot has a separate pressure-regulating valve (see #8), this pin/button will simply raise or drop. But if the pot does not allow you to specify high or low pressure, this pin/button typically has two rings indicating low and high, which will appear as the pressure in the pot rises. In our testing of different pots, we found that on some, this indicator is easy to keep an eye on from a distance; others are more of a hassle, requiring you to hover over the pot in order to monitor the indicator.

The underside of the pressure indicator acts as a regulator and safety mechanism. If there is pressure in the pot, the rubber O-ring at the base of the indicator will seal off the opening and the cooker can't be opened. On some pots if the lid is not properly closed, or if there is too much pressure built up inside the pot, it will also act as a safety valve and allow excess pressure to escape.

8 Pressure Regulating/Steam Release Valve: Some pots have a knob that you turn to low or high (called 1 or I and 2 or II on some pots), which allows you to indicate your target pressure level before you start to bring the pot up to pressure. The pressure indicator (#7) will rise when that pressure level has been reached. This knob typically also acts as a valve to release excess pressure. On our Best Buy pot from Fagor, the steam released during a quick release is let out through this valve. On pots without this high/low setting feature, there is typically a simple steam release valve.

9 Steam Release Points: Depending on the construction of the pot, various points built into the lid allow excess pressure to escape as needed. With some pots, as pressure builds, steam and/or liquid may also be released at these points until the pot is up to pressure.

10 Silicone Gasket: This rubber ring fits snugly in a channel around the perimeter of the underside of the lid. When the lid is in place correctly, the gasket allows an airtight seal to be created, which in turn allows pressure to build within the pot.

11 Safety Vents: These cutouts around the perimeter of the lid allow for release of steam in case of excess pressure. They are usually a backup safety feature that comes into play only if all of the safety valve(s) are blocked with food. In this case, the pressure will tear the gasket and steam will escape through these cutouts.

12 Fill Lines: Depending on the food you are cooking, you should only fill the pot either half or two-thirds full. Some pots have fill lines to help you keep a better eye on this.

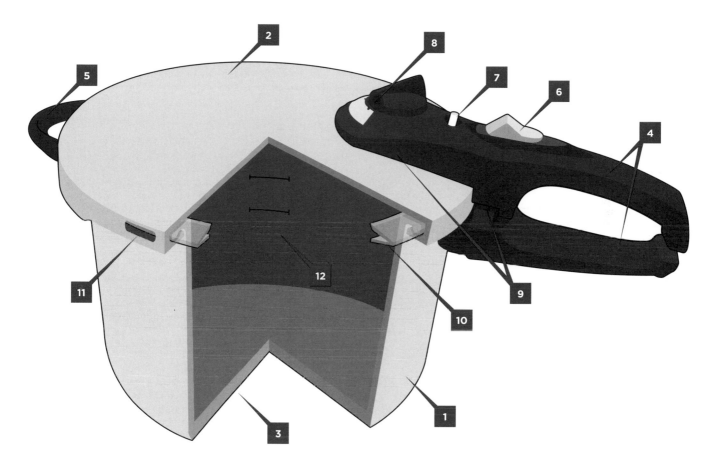

Illustration: Jay Layman

1. Cooking Pot
2. Lid
3. Disk Base
4. Primary Handle
5. Secondary Handle

6. Pressure Safety Lock/Locked Lid Indicator
7. Pressure Indicator
8. Pressure Regulating/Steam Release Valve

9. Steam Release Points
10. Silicone Gasket
11. Safety Vents
12. Fill Lines

Using a Pressure Cooker, Step-by-Step

Pressure cookers are available in electric and stovetop models. Although the recipes in this book, and the following basic procedure, were developed using our Best Buy stovetop model (see the complete testing results on pages 11–13), they will work in both electric and stovetop models. However, we found we had to make some recipe adjustments for the electric models to get good results (see page 14 for an overview; specific adjustments are also noted in the Troubleshooting section of each recipe).

1. BROWN MEAT, THEN AROMATICS: For some of our recipes, we found that browning meat, and sometimes aromatics like onion, garlic, or tomato paste, is important for adding depth. Browning creates flavorful browned bits, also known as fond, on the bottom of the pot. This fond can then be incorporated into the braising liquid (which we often reduce after the pressurized cooking time to make a sauce). Meat is browned in a little oil right in the pot. Since the pressure cooker is so good at maximizing flavor, we have found that browning half of the meat is usually sufficient, rather than browning all of it as we do in conventional recipes. Once the meat is brown, set it aside and brown any aromatics.

2. ADD LIQUID: Once the aromatics are softened, add the liquid to the pot. Liquid is a key player when using a pressure cooker since it, along with any juices that the food might release, will become the steam that creates pressure and cooks the food. It is also key for preventing scorching. Liquid is often in the form of water or broth, but even the liquid from canned tomatoes can be sufficient. When using electric pressure cookers, it's particularly important to use sufficient liquid or else the cooker may not work properly.

3. LOCK THE LID IN PLACE: Follow the manufacturer's instructions to lock the lid of your pressure cooker securely in place on the pot. Different pots have different systems for letting you know the lid is correctly positioned, but generally, you line up a marker on the pot with a marker on the lid, then twist the lid until the two parts of the handle are lined up. Some have an indicator that signifies the lid is properly closed; others have a lock button.

4. BRING THE PRESSURE COOKER TO LOW/HIGH PRESSURE: Once the lid is in place, heat the pot over medium-high heat until the pressure indicator signifies that you have reached the desired pressure level. On some pressure cookers, you have a knob that allows you to select high or low pressure and you simply wait for the pressure indicator to signify your chosen pressure level has been reached. On other pots, the pressure indicator will have markings for low and high pressure that you have to watch for.

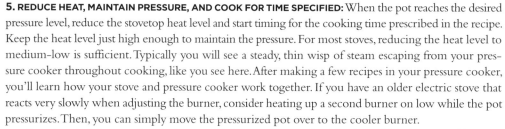

5. REDUCE HEAT, MAINTAIN PRESSURE, AND COOK FOR TIME SPECIFIED: When the pot reaches the desired pressure level, reduce the stovetop heat level and start timing for the cooking time prescribed in the recipe. Keep the heat level just high enough to maintain the pressure. For most stoves, reducing the heat level to medium-low is sufficient. Typically you will see a steady, thin wisp of steam escaping from your pressure cooker throughout cooking, like you see here. After making a few recipes in your pressure cooker, you'll learn how your stove and pressure cooker work together. If you have an older electric stove that reacts very slowly when adjusting the burner, consider heating up a second burner on low while the pot pressurizes. Then, you can simply move the pressurized pot over to the cooler burner.

Keep in mind that running the heat too high not only runs the risk of scorching the pot and burning the food, but it also creates excess pressure within the pot, which then triggers the pot to release pressure through valves and vents. In the worst cases it will tear the gasket (the good news is that with so many safety mechanisms, it won't explode!). But on the flip side, don't turn it down too low or the pressure indicator will drop and the cooking time will be inaccurate.

6. RELEASE THE PRESSURE: Depending on the recipe, you will either let the pressure in the pot release naturally (this takes about 15 minutes), or manually release it quickly.

A. QUICK PRESSURE RELEASE: Today's pressure cookers have a release valve or button that you can use to quickly, easily, and safely release the pressure in the pot (refer to your pressure cooker's user manual to learn how to quick release pressure from your particular model). Just make sure to point the steam vent away from you and anyone else standing nearby before quick releasing the pressure. Some manuals will suggest moving your pot to the sink and running cold water on the lid, but we don't recommend this method, not only because lifting a pot full of food can be awkward and difficult, but if water inadvertently blocks the vents, a vacuum can be created inside the pot and damage your pressure cooker.

B. NATURAL PRESSURE RELEASE: Simply slide the pressurized pot off the heat onto a cold burner; don't do anything to the lid. Let the pot sit for 15 minutes. During this time the pressure will drop naturally. Because food continues to cook as the pressure drops, and because how quickly the pressure releases varies from pot to pot, after 15 minutes we quick release any remaining pressure (at this point, depending on the amount of food in the pot, there may or may not be pressure left in the pot). This keeps the recipe results uniform, no matter the pressure cooker.

7. REMOVE THE LID: Even though the pressure has been released, there will still be some steam in the pressure cooker, and it will rush out when the lid is removed. Carefully unlock and twist the lid to the open position, then lift it up at an angle so that the steam escapes away from you. In many cases, at this point the food is ready to serve. However, in some recipes we continue to cook with the lid off. Sometimes we reduce the braising liquid to create a sauce. In other recipes, we intentionally undercook the food under pressure so that we can finish cooking it to perfect doneness under a watchful eye.

The Test Kitchen Guide to Buying a Pressure Cooker

Today's pressure cookers are easier, quieter, and safer than the old-fashioned jiggle-top models, but not all cookers are created equal. After testing both stovetop and electric models to prepare a variety of recipes, we discovered there are a handful of key traits to evaluate when investing in a pressure cooker. Here is what we learned:

Electric versus stovetop: Electric cookers offer the big advantage that you can set them and walk away. However, they do have some drawbacks:
• Most electric pressure cookers hold 6 quarts, which is fine if you are cooking for four but not good if you want to make larger batches.
• The food cooks in a liner pot with a nonstick coating, which is far less durable than stainless steel stovetop pots. These liner pots are light, slippery, and unanchored, so they spun around as we stirred food. They also lack handles, which made pouring off hot liquid awkward.
• The heating elements on electric models are weaker than those of a stove, so browning can be challenging. To reduce sauces, we found we had to use the browning setting since the simmer and sauté settings weren't hot enough. Cooking liquids down to a certain consistency also took longer in the electric pots.
• Because they switch to the keep-warm mode after cooking, for recipes that call for a quick release you have to return just when cooking is done to vent steam and shut off the pot or your food will overcook. They can also switch to the keep-warm mode when there's not enough liquid, a problem when cooking whole chicken or meatloaf.
• There is a lag between the time the electric pots come up to pressure and when the timer starts, which led to overcooked food when preparing recipes with short cooking times.

• They take up a lot of space compared with stovetop models.
  Given these factors, we prefer stovetop models, but if an electric pressure cooker is what you want, there are two models we recommend with reservations (see page 11).

Size: While 6-quart cookers are popular, we recommend buying an 8-quart because you can always make less food in a bigger pot, but not the other way around. Cooking recipes that serve four is generally not a problem in either size cooker, but when you get to those recipes that involve larger yields, or you want to cook a pound of beans, the recipe simply won't fit in a 6-quart.

Height of pot's sides and size of cooking surface: Low, wide cookers proved better since they provide a generous cooking surface, helping food brown thoroughly and efficiently before the lid is put on the pot. Wide pots also allow for browning meat in fewer batches, and our testers found this shape easier to see and reach into. Straight-sided pots were also easier to clean.

Thickness and breadth of the disk on the pot's bottom: We found that stovetop pressure-cooker pots with a thicker, wider disk retain heat better than those with thinner disks. They quickly reached pressure and allowed for steady, hands-off cooking. Those with thinner, narrower bases forced us to adjust the heat up and down like a yo-yo to maintain pressure.

Ease of use: Some lids lock automatically when the handles are lined up, while others require another step of sliding a switch to manually lock the pot. Some pressure indicators are deep in a hole, making the user lean over the cooker to see them; others are confusing to interpret. The best models we evaluated had pressure indicators that were brightly colored, prominently raised, and easy to read at a glance from several feet away.

Evaporation loss: As a pressure cooker heats up, valves in the lid generally release a trickle of steam until they come to pressure, at which point the pressure indicator rises and should cut off the release of steam. But during our testing, a few continued venting throughout cooking, even if we made sure the pots weren't overpressurized. Losing steam means you are losing some flavor. For recipes that call for a lesser amount of liquid in relation to the cooking time, higher evaporation rates can also translate to scorching. Most recipes call for sufficient quantities of liquid so this shouldn't be a problem, but if you have a cooker with a poor rating for evaporation loss as noted on pages 11–13, or if you own a pot that releases a fair amount of steam, you might consider adding a little extra liquid to the pot.

Maximum temperature reached: Temperature correlates directly with pressure. High pressure is considered to be 15 psi, which is reached when the liquid in the cooker is boiling at 250 degrees. Some cookers never achieved that temperature, and the food wasn't fully cooked in some of the bottom-ranking pots when the time was up.

Rating Electric Pressure Cookers

We tested eight stovetop and four electric models, using each to prepare risotto, chicken stock, beef stew, Boston "baked" beans, and tomato sauce with pork ribs. Since many recipes call for sautéing before cooking under pressure, we checked evenness of browning by cooking crêpes in the pot. We evaluated the overall size, shape, weight, and ease of use. We measured the temperature inside each cooker during 30 minutes at high pressure; pots that came closer to reaching 250 degrees rated higher. We also measured the amount of water lost over the course of 1 hour at high pressure; cookers with lower evaporation levels rated higher.

KEY: GOOD ★★★   FAIR ★★   POOR ★

RECOMMENDED WITH RESERVATIONS

	CRITERIA		TESTERS' COMMENTS
EMERIL 1000-Watt 6-Quart Electric Pressure Cooker by T-fal MODEL: 42EW716 PRICE: $107.90 WEIGHT: 11.7 lb BOTTOM THICKNESS: 2.14 mm COOKING SURFACE DIAMETER: 7¼ in HEIGHT OF SIDES: 6¼ in HIGHEST TEMPERATURE: 245 degrees	COOKING EASE OF USE EVAPORATION LOSS	★★★ ★★ ★★★	Browning was fairly easy and efficient; stewed meats were fork-tender and juicy; baked beans were mahogany, with a tender texture. We'd prefer a larger capacity and handles on the cooking pot to make pouring easier. Sometimes when we started with less than 2 cups of liquid, the pot switched to "keep warm" mode.
CUISINART 1000-Watt 6-Quart Electric Pressure Cooker MODEL: CPC-600 PRICE: $96 WEIGHT: 12.15 lb BOTTOM THICKNESS: 2.5 mm COOKING SURFACE DIAMETER: 7¼ in HEIGHT OF SIDES: 6¼ in HIGHEST TEMPERATURE: 241 degrees	COOKING EASE OF USE EVAPORATION LOSS	★★★ ★★ ★★½	This model is very similar to the Emeril model in design and cooking (food was slightly less stellar but still quite good). It allowed more evaporation, and we would prefer a larger capacity and less-slippery liner. Sometimes when we started with less than 2 cups of liquid, the pot switched to "keep warm" mode.

NOT RECOMMENDED

	CRITERIA		TESTERS' COMMENTS
FAGOR Stainless-Steel 3-in-1 6-Quart Multi-Cooker MODEL: 670040230 PRICE: $89.99 WEIGHT: 11.4 lb BOTTOM THICKNESS: 2.2 mm COOKING SURFACE DIAMETER: 7½ in HEIGHT OF SIDES: 6¼ in HIGHEST TEMPERATURE: 234 degrees	COOKING EASE OF USE EVAPORATION LOSS	★½ ★½ ★	While we recommended this model with reservations in the past, we have since found pots that perform better. Tomato sauce scorched, and we noticed black sheets of burned sauce were released from the nonstick pot. The capacity was a drawback, and the slippery pot was difficult to grasp when pouring stock.
MAXI-MATIC Elite 8-Quart Electric Pressure Cooker MODEL: EPC-808 PRICE: $104.30 WEIGHT: 15 lb BOTTOM THICKNESS: 2.3 mm COOKING SURFACE DIAMETER: 8 in HEIGHT OF SIDES: 6¾ in HIGHEST TEMPERATURE: 239 degrees	COOKING EASE OF USE EVAPORATION LOSS	★ ½ ★★½	We had high hopes for this 8-quart cooker, but they were quickly dashed. The gasket is a pain to replace after cleaning, and the bottom of the pot became stained and the coating felt worn after cooking tomato sauce. Its control panel is poor, and it often shut off while we were sautéing. The crêpe test revealed uneven browning.

Rating Stovetop Pressure Cookers

KEY: GOOD ★★★   FAIR ★★   POOR ★

HIGHLY RECOMMENDED	CRITERIA		TESTERS' COMMENTS
FISSLER Vitaquick 8-Liter (8½-Quart) Pressure Cooker MODEL: 600 700N 08 079 PRICE: $279.95 WEIGHT: 8.95 lb BOTTOM THICKNESS: 7.24 mm COOKING SURFACE DIAMETER: 9 in HEIGHT OF SIDES: 6½ in HIGHEST TEMPERATURE: 253 degrees	COOKING EASE OF USE EVAPORATION LOSS	★★★ ★★★ ★★★	Solidly constructed, with a low, wide profile that made browning foods easy, this well-engineered cooker has an automatic lock and an easy-to-monitor pressure valve. The only cooker to reach 250 degrees at high pressure, it cooked food to perfection in the time range suggested by the recipes.
FAGOR Duo 8-Quart Stainless Steel Pressure Cooker MODEL: 918060787 PRICE: $99.95 WEIGHT: 6.85 lb BOTTOM THICKNESS: 7.15 mm COOKING SURFACE DIAMETER: 9 in HEIGHT OF SIDES: 6¾ in HIGHEST TEMPERATURE: 246 degrees **BEST BUY**	COOKING EASE OF USE EVAPORATION LOSS	★★★ ★★★ ★★★	Performing much like our winner at a fraction of the price (though lighter and less smooth to latch), this cooker has low sides and a broad cooking surface; its pressure indicator and dial are easy to monitor. Falling just short of the 250-degree target, it performs well nonetheless.

RECOMMENDED			
PRESTO 8-Quart Stainless Steel Pressure Cooker MODEL: 01370 PRICE: $64.54 WEIGHT: 6.2 lb BOTTOM THICKNESS: 4.76 mm COOKING SURFACE DIAMETER: 8½ in HEIGHT OF SIDES: 7 in HIGHEST TEMPERATURE: 249 degrees	COOKING EASE OF USE EVAPORATION LOSS	★★½ ★★ ★★★	The lowest-priced cooker in our lineup, this flimsier model has a hard-to-monitor recessed pressure indicator and bulging sides that encourage scorching. Still, its low, wide profile was good for browning and stirring; it cooked meats and beans well. This model has no low-pressure setting, a drawback if you want to cook certain rice, grains, and beans.
TRAMONTINA 8-Quart Heavy-Duty Pressure Cooker MODEL: 80130500 PRICE: $99.95 WEIGHT: 6.7 lb BOTTOM THICKNESS: 5.19 mm COOKING SURFACE DIAMETER: 7¾ in HEIGHT OF SIDES: 7¾ in HIGHEST TEMPERATURE: 243 degrees	COOKING EASE OF USE EVAPORATION LOSS	★★½ ★★ ★★	A narrower cooking surface forced us to brown meat in more batches, but the red pressure indicator was simple to monitor and its controls are straightforward. The cooker didn't reach 250 degrees, so we wound up with slightly too-firm beans, beef, and risotto.

RECOMMENDED WITH RESERVATIONS	CRITERIA		TESTERS' COMMENTS
KUHN RIKON Duromatic 8-Liter Stock Pot Pressure Cooker MODEL: KU3326 PRICE: $179.99 WEIGHT: 6.25 lb BOTTOM THICKNESS: 7.09 mm COOKING SURFACE DIAMETER: 8¼ in HEIGHT OF SIDES: 8¼ in HIGHEST TEMPERATURE: 240 degrees	COOKING EASE OF USE EVAPORATION LOSS	★★ ★★½ ★	This cooker's small disk bottom caused scorching and forced us to keep flames low, delaying reaching pressure. It is deeper and narrower than we prefer. The pressure indicator was easy to monitor, though it often dipped, forcing us to hover to adjust the temperature. That said, this model produced tender beans and stew.
FAGOR Futuro 6-Quart Pressure Cooker MODEL: 918013142 PRICE: $95.73 WEIGHT: 6.10 lb BOTTOM THICKNESS: 4.64 mm COOKING SURFACE DIAMETER: 8 in HEIGHT OF SIDES: 6⅛ in HIGHEST TEMPERATURE: 238 degrees	COOKING EASE OF USE EVAPORATION LOSS	★½ ★ ★★½	While this pot's design was light and maneuverable, with a low, wide shape, its 6-quart capacity (the biggest size available) was a drawback. Bulging sides hang over the disk bottom, leading to scorching. Beans and beef weren't properly tender at the end of cooking time.

NOT RECOMMENDED

	CRITERIA		TESTERS' COMMENTS
MAGEFESA Practika Plus Stainless Steel 8-Quart Super Fast Pressure Cooker MODEL: 010PPRAPL75 PRICE: $77.84 WEIGHT: 6.55 lb BOTTOM THICKNESS: 6.19 mm COOKING SURFACE DIAMETER: 7½ in HEIGHT OF SIDES: 8 in HIGHEST TEMPERATURE: 230 degrees	COOKING EASE OF USE EVAPORATION LOSS	★½ ★ ★★	With a tall, moderately narrow pot that overhangs its even narrower disk bottom and a hard-to-interpret, recessed pressure indicator, this model created extra work. Its valves made odd noises; it sometimes struggled to retain pressure and took longer than other cookers to make tender beef stew and beans.
WMF Perfect Plus 8½-Quart Pressure Cooker MODEL: 07.9314.9300 PRICE: $246.99 WEIGHT: 7.95 lb BOTTOM THICKNESS: 5.38 mm COOKING SURFACE DIAMETER: 7½ in HEIGHT OF SIDES: 9 in HIGHEST TEMPERATURE: 247 degrees	COOKING EASE OF USE EVAPORATION LOSS	★½ ½ ★★½	While solidly built, this cooker had a tall, narrow shape that made more work, as did its fussy extra valve. One sample stopped working properly halfway through testing. The food wasn't bad, but it was not worth the effort. For the price, this cooker should be perfect.

Tips for Pressure Cooker Success

GET TO KNOW YOUR PRESSURE COOKER: Read the user's manual before using your pressure cooker, as it will have instructions specific to your cooker that we don't cover.

BE FAMILIAR WITH YOUR STOVE WHEN USING A STOVETOP PRESSURE COOKER: While we call for medium-low heat once pressure is reached, your burner may need to be set higher or lower to maintain pressure. Electric burners cool down more slowly than gas, so consider moving to a different burner once pressure is reached.

ADD EXACTLY THE AMOUNT OF LIQUID THE RECIPE INDICATES: A pressure cooker depends on some liquid inside the pot to cook the food. Frequently it's a combination of liquid added directly to the pot and juices released by the food itself. Remember there's no evaporation, so you don't need much. Most manuals recommend a set minimum amount of liquid, but we found during our testing the amount you have to add actually varies depending on the food in the pot and the exact cooking time.

KEEP TRACK OF TIME AS SOON AS THE REQUIRED PRESSURE LEVEL IS REACHED: Since food is being cooked at 250 degrees, a minute can make a huge difference when cooking under pressure. Always follow the recipe's cooking times exactly. Time begins when the pot is up to pressure; time stops when you begin the quick or natural release.

USE ONLY THE RELEASE TYPE INDICATED IN THE RECIPE: If we specify quick release, don't change it to natural release, and vice versa. The release type factors into the cooking time, and the final result will be altered (for the worse) if you change the release.

YOUR PRESSURE COOKER IS NOT FOR EVERYTHING: You may have fallen in love with your pressure cooker, but quick-cooking foods like asparagus and fish fillets are fine (and plenty efficient) when prepared using conventional cooking methods.

ADJUST RECIPES FOR AN ELECTRIC PRESSURE COOKER: We tested each recipe in both a stovetop and an electric pot and found electrics always required a few adjustments.
1. To reduce sauces, use the browning setting, not the simmer setting.
2. For recipes with a cooking time of 10 minutes or less, use your own timer rather than the built-in timer, and start time as soon as the pot comes up to pressure.
3. Never let the cooker switch to the keep-warm setting. For recipes that call for a quick release, release the pressure immediately after the pressurized cooking time; for recipes that require a natural release, turn the cooker off immediately after the pressurized cooking time and let the pressure release naturally for 15 minutes.
4. You may need to add about 1 cup more liquid before cooking under pressure, then simmer to thicken sauces to proper consistency before serving.

SAFETY AND CLEANING

- Before you begin, make sure the rubber gasket in the lid is in place and in good shape (soft and springy, not dry or cracked). They wear out over time, so if your gasket seems brittle like an old rubber band, it's time to replace it.

- Use only a gasket made to fit your exact brand and size cooker; they are not standardized. You can order replacement gaskets (and other parts) directly from the manufacturer.

- After each use, remove and clean the gasket and rub it with vegetable oil to keep it in good shape.

- Clean the vents and inspect valves before and after every use. Make sure the valves aren't clogged, especially after cooking foaming, starchy foods such as rice and beans. If the valves seem sticky or hard to move, dismantle the valve assembly and clean all the pieces, following your manual's instructions. If this doesn't solve the problem, the entire valve unit should be replaced. Also be sure to check the nut that secures the valve assembly to the inside of the lid and tighten it if needed.

- Don't overfill your cooker— keep food levels at or below the maximum (two-thirds full for most recipes except for foaming and expanding foods, in which case the pot should be only half full).

- When quick-releasing pressure, learn the direction in which your cooker vents the hot steam and keep this pointed away from yourself and others.

Pressure Cooker Troubleshooting Guide

When you run into problems using a pressure cooker, those issues can't be fixed with the same familiar techniques you might use when roasting in the oven or simmering on the stovetop—you can't take off the lid for a peek, or adjust the heat up or down without serious consequences. After spending months in the kitchen with our pressure cookers, we came up with a few key tricks to fix the common problems we ran into.

Problem: Scorching
Solution: Use enough liquid and scrape up browned bits.
Scorching can happen to anyone on occasion, but to limit the incidents, we made sure there was always enough liquid in the pot, especially for recipes with longer pressurized cooking times. Also, be sure to scrape up any browned bits (fond) left from browning before putting the pot under pressure.

Problem: Pressure Loss During Cooking
Solution: Turn up the heat, then back it off.
When using a stovetop pressure cooker, it's normal to adjust the heat level a few times during cooking in order to maintain pressure. If the pot loses pressure, simply turn the heat back to medium-high to restore the pressure as quickly as possible, then turn the heat back down to prevent scorching.

Problem: Uneven Cooking
Solution: Prep ingredients as directed.
Whenever we came across unevenly cooked beans, rice, stew, or roast, we could always trace the problem back to ingredients that were inaccurately measured or badly prepped. Buy the right size roast or chicken, measure liquids accurately, and grab a ruler when prepping vegetables.

Problem: Undercooked Food
Solution: Continue to simmer the food gently on the stovetop.
Since it's impossible to test the doneness of food as it cooks under pressure, sometimes food might be slightly underdone. We intentionally undercook some foods so we can monitor them as they finish. Simply finish the recipe by gently simmering it, adding extra liquid as needed.

Problem: Sauce is too thick, or too thin
Solution: Add additional liquid, or continue to simmer.
There are a lot of variables that affect the texture of a sauce, including your stove's heat level and freshness of ingredients. Sauces that are too thin can simply be simmered uncovered on the stovetop to thicken up before serving, and thick sauces can be thinned out with additional broth or water.

PRESSURE COOKING AT HIGH ALTITUDE

At high altitudes, there is less oxygen and atmospheric pressure, which means liquids evaporate faster and boil at lower temperatures than they do at sea level. Because of this, when you are using traditional cooking methods above 2,000 feet, you have to compensate for that lower boiling point by increasing the cooking time—turning up the heat won't help the food cook faster since no matter how high the cooking temperature goes, water cannot exceed its own boiling point. That is, unless you are using a pressure cooker.

Cooking under pressure at high altitude is a great timesaving tool, but many manufacturers still suggest adjusting the cooking time slightly to account for the atmospheric difference. If your pressure cooker manual doesn't include instructions about cooking at high altitude, call the manufacturer directly or check their website for instructions.

The basic formula most manufacturers follow is to increase cooking times 5 percent for every 1,000 feet you are located above 2,000 feet above sea level. For example, if a recipe indicates the cooking-under-pressure time is 40 minutes and you are at 3,000 feet above sea level, you would increase the time to 42 minutes (5 percent longer); if you are at 4,000 feet above sea level, you would increase the time under pressure to 44 minutes (10 percent longer). You may have to add a little more liquid to compensate for the longer cooking time.

Cooking Rice and Grains in a Pressure Cooker

Charts for cooking rice and grains in a pressure cooker abound, but one month, more than 100 tests, and 74 pounds of grains and rice later, we found existing methods and times faulty. So we started from scratch.

Our philosophy was to aim for slightly underdone, then finish by simmering for the last few minutes uncovered, which allowed us to easily check for perfect doneness. We found this method was critical to account for variations among different pressure cookers, age of grains, and the simple fact that you just can't test grains along the way as they cook under pressure.

Also, some grains just don't work under pressure: We tried cooking buckwheat, bulgur, millet, and amaranth in the pressure cooker, but even with the most minimal cooking time, these quick-cooking grains were well overdone.

You can serve these rice and grains hot or cold. It's easy to jazz them up by stirring in butter or olive oil, fresh herbs, a splash of lemon juice or vinegar, or other flavorful ingredients such as olives, chopped sun-dried tomatoes, toasted nuts, and/or grated Parmesan.

The instructions on page 17 work for both 6- and 8-quart stovetop models.

WHAT WE LEARNED

Rinse rice and grains: Grains and rice are typically coated with a thin dusting of starch. This coating needs to be rinsed away before cooking or else the rice/grains clump together, and the cooking water turns starchy and foamy, potentially causing the pressure valve to clog.

Soaking some grains is a plus: Soaking shortens the cooking time for some longer-cooking grains and can help prevent them from blowing out. However, it's not a must; you can cook unsoaked grains, it will just take longer and you will see a few more blowouts.

Always add a little oil: Adding oil when cooking both rice and grains helps the individual grains remain more distinct and clump less. Oil also helps reduce the amount of starchy foam.

Don't forget a little salt: Adding salt to the pot prior to cooking adds flavor, but it's crucial to measure carefully, especially in the case of grains. For grains, we found too much salt slows down the cooking time and makes the centers of the grains too firm. (This was particularly noticeable with wheat berries.)

Use enough water: Having enough water in the pot proved crucial for even cooking. The amount also affects the time it takes for the pot to come to pressure and the cooking time; don't be tempted to adjust the water amounts.

Use low pressure if you can: While cooking rice and grains on high pressure worked in most cases, we preferred low pressure. Using low pressure generally resulted in fewer blown out grains. Unfortunately, some pressure cookers don't have a low setting, so we also list the cooking times for high pressure. For rice and grains with a cooking time of 5 minutes or less, we found no difference in cooking time between high and low.

The release type matters: For rice and grains, we generally prefer natural release because it guards against blowouts and prevents foam from spraying out of the vent. Rice and grains with very short cooking times are an exception since a natural release would lead to overcooking (given their short cooking times, excessive foam wasn't an issue anyway). Keep in mind that release types and cooking times go hand in hand; don't be tempted to swap release types as it will dramatically affect the results.

Adjust if using a 6-quart electric pot: Always use low pressure and do not use the pot's built-in timer since it usually has a delayed start. Instead, use your own timer and start the countdown as soon as the pot comes to pressure. For cooking times longer than 5 minutes, be sure to turn the cooker off immediately after the cooking time and let the pressure release naturally for 15 minutes; do not let the cooker switch to the warm setting. For cooking times shorter than 5 minutes, just bring the pot to low pressure, then immediately quick release the pressure.

SOAKING GRAINS

If you choose to soak longer-cooking grains, follow this procedure: Dissolve 2½ teaspoons salt in 2 quarts cold water in large bowl or container. Add 1 cup rinsed grains and let soak at room temperature for at least 8 hours, or up to 24 hours. Drain and cook as directed.

RINSING RICE AND GRAINS

Place rice/grains in fine-mesh strainer and rinse under cool water until water runs clear, occasionally stirring with your hand. Set strainer over bowl and let rice/grains drain until needed.

COOKING INSTRUCTIONS

Rinse rice/grains, then combine with 1 tablespoon oil in pressure cooker pot. Stir in salt and 3 quarts water and lock pressure-cooker lid in place. Bring to desired pressure over medium-high heat. As soon as pot reaches pressure, reduce heat to medium-low and cook as directed in chart, adjusting heat as needed to maintain pressure level. Remove pot from heat. Release pressure as directed in chart, then carefully remove lid, allowing steam to escape away from you. Taste for doneness, and simmer gently over medium heat as needed until tender. Drain cooked rice/grains through fine-mesh strainer. Makes about 3 cups.

RICE / GRAIN	AMOUNT	SALT	PRESSURE LEVEL	COOKING TIME	RELEASE TYPE
Sushi Rice	1 cup	1½ tsp	Low or High	3 minutes	Quick
Arborio Rice	1 cup	1½ tsp	Low or High	2 minutes	Quick
Medium-Grain White Rice	1 cup	1½ tsp	Low or High	2 minutes	Quick
Long-Grain White Rice	1 cup	1½ tsp	Low or High	3 minutes	Quick
Basmati Rice	1 cup	1½ tsp	Low or High	2 minutes	Quick
Jasmine Rice	1 cup	1½ tsp	Low or High	1 minute	Quick
Texmati Rice	1 cup	1½ tsp	Low or High	2 minutes	Quick
Short-Grain Brown Rice	1 cup	1½ tsp	Low	15 minutes	Natural
	1 cup	1½ tsp	High	14 minutes	Natural
Medium-Grain Brown Rice	1 cup	1½ tsp	Low	8 minutes	Natural
	1 cup	1½ tsp	High	6 minutes	Natural
Long-Grain Brown Rice	1 cup	1½ tsp	Low	13 minutes	Natural
	1 cup	1½ tsp	High	12 minutes	Natural
Brown Texmati Rice	1 cup	1½ tsp	Low	10 minutes	Natural
	1 cup	1½ tsp	High	9 minutes	Natural
Wild Rice	1 cup	1½ tsp	Low	22 minutes	Natural
	1 cup	1½ tsp	High	18 minutes	Natural
Quinoa	1 cup	¼ tsp	Low or High	1 minute	Quick
Red Quinoa	1 cup	¼ tsp	Low or High	5 minutes	Quick
Farro	1 cup	¼ tsp	Low	7 minutes	Natural
	1 cup	¼ tsp	High	6 minutes	Natural
Pearl Barley	1 cup	¼ tsp	Low or High	10 minutes	Natural
	1 cup, soaked	¼ tsp	Low or High	1 minute	Natural
Kamut	1 cup	¼ tsp	Low	35 minutes	Natural
	1 cup	¼ tsp	High	34 minutes	Natural
	1 cup, soaked	¼ tsp	Low	15 minutes	Natural
	1 cup, soaked	¼ tsp	High	14 minutes	Natural
Wheat Berries	1 cup	¼ tsp	Low	27 minutes	Natural
	1 cup	¼ tsp	High	25 minutes	Natural
	1 cup, soaked	¼ tsp	Low	12 minutes	Natural
	1 cup, soaked	¼ tsp	High	10 minutes	Natural

Cooking Beans in a Pressure Cooker

We prefer the flavor and texture of dried beans to canned, and the pressure cooker proves itself truly invaluable here since it can cook dried beans in a fraction of their conventional cooking time. We cooked almost 150 pounds of dried beans to find the best method and foolproof timing. It proved best to aim for slightly underdone beans, then finish by simmering for the last few minutes uncovered on the stovetop so we could more easily check for doneness. This method accounts for variations among pressure cookers, the age of the beans, and the simple fact that you can't test the beans along the way.

TYPE OF BEAN	PRESSURE LEVEL	COOK TIME
Black Beans	Low	10 min
	High	9 min
Black-Eyed Peas	Low or High	5 min
Cannellini Beans	Low or High	5 min
Garbanzo	Low or High	3 min
Great Northern Beans	Low or High	5 min
Navy Beans	Low	10 min
	High	8 min
Pinto Beans	Low or High	3 min
Red Kidney Beans	Low or High	5 min
Flageolet Beans	Low	10 min
	High	9 min
Cranberry Beans	Low	9 min
	High	8 min

WHAT WE LEARNED

Soak beans overnight before cooking: Soaking beans before cooking is crucial for even cooking and to minimize busted beans.

Add salt and oil: Adding salt to the soaking liquid and the cooking liquid tenderizes the beans' skins, dramatically reducing the number of beans that burst. Adding oil to the cooking liquid prevents foaming.

Use low pressure and a natural release: We had slightly better results cooking beans under low pressure. But high pressure works OK if that's the only setting your pot has. A natural release helps the beans retain their shape, and it doesn't spray a mess of foam out of the vent like a quick release does.

Skim the floaters: Sometimes we noticed a few beans floating on top of the water after releasing the pressure and removing the lid. These beans typically turned out underdone so it's best to fish them out of the pot.

Adjust if using a 6-quart stovetop pot: Cook only half batches of beans (½ pound beans, 2 quarts water, ½ tablespoon oil, and ½ teaspoon salt) and shorten the cooking times by 2 minutes.

Adjust if using a 6-quart electric pot: Cook only half batches of beans (½ pound beans, 2 quarts water, ½ tablespoon oil, and ½ teaspoon salt). Use low pressure, and do not use the pot's built-in timer. Instead, use your own timer and start the countdown as soon as the pot comes to pressure. For cooking times longer than 5 minutes, reduce the cooking time by 2 minutes. For cooking times shorter than 5 minutes, just bring the pot up to low pressure. To naturally release the pressure, turn the cooker off immediately after the cooking time and let it sit for 15 minutes; do not let the cooker switch to the warm setting.

SOAKING BEANS
Dissolve 2 tablespoons salt into 4 quarts water. Add 1 pound beans, rinsed and picked over, and soak at room temperature for 8 to 24 hours. Drain and rinse beans.

COOKING INSTRUCTIONS
Combine 1 pound soaked beans with 1 tablespoon vegetable oil in pressure-cooker pot; stir to coat beans. Add 4 quarts water and 1 teaspoon salt. Lock pressure-cooker lid in place and bring to desired pressure over medium-high heat. As soon as pot reaches pressure, reduce heat to medium-low and cook as directed in chart, adjusting heat as needed to maintain pressure. Remove pot from heat and allow pressure to release naturally for 15 minutes. Quick release any remaining pressure, then carefully remove lid, allowing steam to escape away from you. Skim any beans floating on top of water and discard. Taste beans for doneness; simmer beans gently over medium heat as needed until tender. Drain beans, discarding cooking liquid.

Cooking Meat in a Pressure Cooker

Through our exhaustive testing of the recipes in this book, we learned a lot about which meats are well suited to cooking under pressure and which are not. We had great luck pressure cooking all types of chicken, but the same can not be said for beef and pork. In general, we found that the cuts of pork and beef commonly used for braising or barbecue work best in a pressure cooker, although pork tenderloin and beef sirloin roast are two notable exceptions (with a few tricks, they turned out incredibly well when cooked under pressure).

To help you translate one of your own stovetop recipes to the pressure cooker, the chart at right contains a list of meats we think work well in a pressure cooker along with their relative cooking times and preferred release type. These times are just a starting point and can vary depending on how you cut the meat and what else you add to the pot.

These instructions work for 6- and 8-quart models. For 6-quart electric models, use your own timer when cooking cuts with a pressurized cooking time of 10 minutes or less, and start the countdown as soon as the pot comes to pressure. Also, when a quick release is required, release the pressure immediately after the pressurized cooking time; do not let an electric cooker switch to the warm setting.

CUT OF MEAT	COOK TIME (AT HIGH PRESSURE)	RELEASE TYPE
Poultry		
4 (6- to 8-ounce) Boneless, Skinless Chicken Breasts	8 minutes	Quick
4 (10½- to 15-ounce) Bone-in Split Chicken Breasts	15 minutes	Quick
8 (3-ounce) Boneless Chicken Thighs	20 minutes	Quick
8 (5- to 7-ounce) Bone-in Chicken Thighs	20 minutes	Quick
4 pounds Chicken Wings	10 minutes	Quick
1 (4-pound) Whole Chicken	25 minutes	Quick
1 (4½- to 5½-pound) Whole Chicken	35 minutes	Quick
1 (6-pound) Bone-in Turkey Breast	35 minutes	Quick
Ground Meat		
1 pound Ground Turkey, Pork, or Beef	10 minutes	Natural
Stew Meat		
3 pounds Boneless Country-Style Pork Ribs, cut into 1-inch pieces	15 minutes	Natural
3 pounds Boneless Pork Butt, cut into 1-inch pieces	30 minutes	Natural
3 pounds Boneless Beef Short Ribs, cut into 1-inch pieces	25 minutes	Natural
3 pounds Boneless Beef Chuck Roast, cut into 1-inch pieces	25 minutes	Natural
3 pounds Boneless Leg of Lamb, cut into 1-inch pieces	30 minutes	Natural
Roasts		
2 (12- to 16-ounce) Pork Tenderloin	Less than 1 minute	Natural
1 (4-pound) Boneless Pork Butt	1½ hours	Natural
1 (3-pound) Boneless Beef Top Sirloin Roast	20 minutes	Natural
1 (2- to 4-pound) Beef Brisket	1½ hours	Natural
1 (3- to 4-pound) Boneless Beef Chuck-Eye Roast	1½ hours	Natural
Ribs and Veal Shanks		
2 (1½- to 2-pound) racks Pork Baby Back Ribs, cut into 2-rib sections	30 minutes	Natural
6 (12-ounce) Bone-in Beef Short Ribs	1¼ hours	Natural
6 (8-ounce) Boneless Beef Short Ribs	30 minutes	Natural
6 (6- to 10-ounce) Osso Buco-Style Veal Shanks	1 hour	Natural

Cooking Vegetables in a Pressure Cooker

You could theoretically cook any type of vegetable in the pressure cooker. But many vegetables are quite delicate, cook quickly, and retain better flavor and texture using conventional methods. We think cooking only sturdier vegetables that require longer cooking times makes sense in a pressure cooker. So you won't find green beans, broccoli, or zucchini in our chart. What we do include are vegetables like winter squashes, winter greens, and root vegetables such as potatoes, beets, and carrots.

These instructions work for 6- and 8-quart models. For 6-quart electric models, use your own timer when cooking vegetables with a pressurized cooking time of 10 minutes or less, and start the countdown as soon as the pot comes to pressure. Also, quick release the pressure immediately after the pressurized cooking time; do not let the cooker switch to the warm setting.

COOKING INSTRUCTIONS
Combine water and vegetables in pressure-cooker pot. Lock pressure-cooker lid in place and bring to high pressure over medium-high heat. As soon as pot reaches high pressure, reduce heat to medium-low and cook as directed in chart, adjusting heat as needed to maintain high pressure. Remove pot from heat. Quick release pressure, then carefully remove lid, allowing steam to escape away from you. Drain vegetables and season as desired.

VEGETABLE	PREP	WATER	COOK TIME (AT HIGH PRESSURE)	RELEASE TYPE
1 Acorn Squash	scrubbed, cut into 8 wedges, seeded	1 cup	10 minutes	Quick
4 Artichokes	stemmed, top ¼ removed, leaf tips trimmed	1 cup	15 minutes	Quick
8 Baby Artichokes	stemmed, top ¼ removed	1 cup	5 minutes	Quick
6 Beets	halved if small or quartered if large	1 cup	20 minutes	Quick
1 pound Brussels Sprouts	halved	1 cup	2 minutes	Quick
1 Butternut Squash	peeled, seeded, cut into 1-inch pieces	1 cup	12 minutes	Quick
1 head Red or Green Cabbage	cut into 8 wedges	1 quart	15 minutes	Quick
1 pound Carrots	peeled, cut into ½-inch pieces	1 cup	4 minutes	Quick
1 head Cauliflower	cored, cut into 1-inch pieces	1 cup	2 minutes	Quick
	cored, left whole	1 cup	5 minutes	Quick
2 pounds Collard Greens	stemmed, leaves chopped	1 quart	10 minutes	Quick
2 pounds Kale	stemmed, leaves chopped	1 quart	7 minutes	Quick
1 pound Red Potatoes, for salad	scrubbed, cut into ¾-inch pieces	1½ cups plus 2 tablespoons vinegar	7 minutes	Quick
2 pounds Red Potatoes, whole or for smashing	scrubbed, left whole	1 quart	13 minutes	Quick
2 pounds Russet or Yukon Gold Potatoes, for mashing	peeled, sliced ½ inch thick	1 cup	8 minutes	Quick
2 pounds Sweet Potatoes, for mashing	peeled, sliced ½ inch thick	1 cup	15 minutes	Quick

Cooking Broths in a Pressure Cooker

Preparing broths in the pressure cooker is not only faster than conventional methods, but the flavor is also significantly better. The intense heat promotes the extraction of flavor compounds from bones, skin, and vegetables, and in the case of chicken and beef broths, encourages the breakdown of proteins into peptides, which produces noticeably rich meatiness. If using a 6-quart stovetop or electric pressure cooker, make only a half-batch of beef broth, as it will overfill the pot. Chicken and vegetable broth will fill a 6-quart pot two-thirds full; no additional alterations are needed if using a 6-quart electric pressure cooker.

CHICKEN BROTH

MAKES **3 QUARTS**
TOTAL TIME **ABOUT 1¾ HOURS**
PRESSURE LEVEL **HIGH**
RELEASE **QUICK**
TIME UNDER PRESSURE **1 HOUR**

INGREDIENTS

- 1 **tablespoon vegetable oil**
- 3 **pounds bone-in chicken pieces (leg quarters, backs, and/or wings), hacked with meat cleaver into 2-inch pieces**
- 1 **onion, chopped**
- 3 **garlic cloves, lightly crushed, skins discarded**
- 3 **quarts water**
- 1 **teaspoon salt**
- 3 **bay leaves**

1. BUILD FLAVOR: Heat oil in pressure-cooker pot over medium-high heat until smoking. Brown half of chicken on all sides, about 6 minutes; transfer to bowl. Repeat with remaining chicken; transfer to bowl.

2. Pour off all but 1 tablespoon fat left in pot, add onion, and cook over medium heat until softened and well browned, 8 to 10 minutes. Stir in garlic and cook until fragrant, about 30 seconds. Stir in

MAKING CHICKEN BROTH IN A PRESSURE COOKER

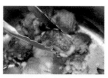
A number of recipes recommend roasting the chicken parts first for both color and flavor. To mimic this effect without requiring the extra hours of work, we simply brown the chicken in the pot before browning the onion and adding the vegetables and water.

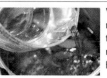
We learned that getting the amount of water just right and nailing the cooking time were crucial elements. Using more than 3 quarts water creates a watery broth, but any less means a skimpy yield. As for the time, we found it takes a full hour to extract all the flavor from the bones and meat.

Once the broth is finished, you need to strain off the solids. Be sure to press firmly on the solids in the strainer to extract as much liquid as possible. After you strain out the solids, you can strain the broth again to make it less cloudy if desired.

1 cup water and scrape up all browned bits from bottom of pot using wooden spoon. Stir in remaining 11 cups water, salt, bay leaves, and browned chicken with any accumulated juices.

3. HIGH PRESSURE FOR 1 HOUR: Lock pressure-cooker lid in place and bring to high pressure over medium-high heat. As soon as pot reaches high pressure, reduce heat to medium-low and cook for 1 hour, adjusting heat as needed to maintain high pressure.

4. QUICK RELEASE PRESSURE: Remove pot from heat. Quick release pressure, then carefully remove lid, allowing steam to escape away from you.

5. Strain broth through fine-mesh strainer into clean container, pressing on solids to extract as much liquid as possible; discard solids. Using large spoon, skim excess fat from surface of broth. (Broth can be refrigerated for up to 2 days, or frozen for several months.)

BEEF BROTH

MAKES **3 QUARTS**
TOTAL TIME **ABOUT 2 HOURS**
PRESSURE LEVEL **HIGH**
RELEASE **QUICK**
TIME UNDER PRESSURE **1½ HOURS**

INGREDIENTS

  3   **pounds beef bones**
  1   **tablespoon vegetable oil**
  1   **onion, chopped**
  1   **carrot, peeled and chopped**
  1   **celery rib, chopped**
  3   **tablespoons tomato paste**
  ¾   **cup dry red wine**
  3   **quarts water**
  1   **pound white mushrooms,**
      trimmed and halved
  2   **tablespoons soy sauce**
  1   **teaspoon salt**
  3   **bay leaves**

1. BUILD FLAVOR: Arrange beef bones on paper towel–lined plate and microwave until well browned, 8 to 10 minutes.

2. Heat oil in pressure-cooker pot over medium heat until shimmering. Stir in onion, carrot, and celery and cook until softened and well browned, 8 to 10 minutes. Stir in tomato paste and cook until fragrant, about 30 seconds. Stir in wine and scrape up all browned bits from bottom of pot using wooden spoon. Stir in water, mushrooms, soy sauce, salt, bay leaves, and microwaved beef bones.

MAKING BEEF BROTH IN A PRESSURE COOKER

For beef broth with a rich flavor, you need to use beef bones, which can be found in most supermarkets. Roasting the bones first will provide color and deep meaty flavor to the broth, but roasting in the oven can take hours. We turn to the microwave, where they brown in just 10 minutes.

A splash of red wine does wonders for the color of the finished broth, and it also adds some welcome acidity. There is no reason to use a fancy or expensive bottle of wine here. Any $8 to $10 bottle of red wine will work just fine.

In addition to onion, celery, and carrots, we also add mushrooms, tomato paste, and soy sauce to the pot to make the broth deeper and more rounded. Each of these has a meaty flavor that enhances the broth.

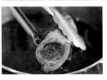

In contrast to our chicken and vegetable broths, we found a longer cooking time was beneficial since it gave the bones more time to release their flavor into the pot. These big bones can get in the way when straining the finished broth, so remove them from the pot before straining.

TROUBLESHOOTING

For a 6-quart pot   Reduce all ingredients by half; cooking time remains the same.

3. HIGH PRESSURE FOR 1½ HOURS: Lock pressure-cooker lid in place and bring to high pressure over medium-high heat. As soon as pot reaches high pressure, reduce heat to medium-low and cook for 1½ hours, adjusting heat as needed to maintain high pressure.

4. QUICK RELEASE PRESSURE: Remove pot from heat. Quick release pressure, then carefully remove lid, allowing steam to escape away from you.

5. Remove and discard bones, letting excess broth drain back into pot. Strain broth through fine-mesh strainer into clean container, pressing on solids to extract as much liquid as possible; discard solids. Using large spoon, skim excess fat from surface of broth. (Broth can be refrigerated for up to 2 days, or frozen for several months.)

VEGETABLE BROTH

MAKES **3 QUARTS**
TOTAL TIME **ABOUT 1½ HOURS**
PRESSURE LEVEL **HIGH**
RELEASE **QUICK**
TIME UNDER PRESSURE **1 HOUR**

INGREDIENTS

1	tablespoon vegetable oil
3	onions, chopped
2	carrots, peeled and chopped
2	celery ribs, chopped
15	garlic cloves, lightly crushed, skins discarded
3	quarts water
½	head cauliflower (1 pound), cored and chopped
1	tomato, cored and chopped
4	scallions, chopped
8	fresh thyme sprigs
1½	teaspoons salt
1	teaspoon black peppercorns
3	bay leaves

1. BUILD FLAVOR: Heat oil in pressure-cooker pot over medium heat until shimmering. Add onions, carrots, and celery and cook until softened and well browned, 8 to 10 minutes. Stir in garlic and cook until fragrant, about 30 seconds. Stir in 1 cup water and scrape up all browned bits from bottom of pot using wooden spoon. Stir in remaining 11 cups water, cauliflower, tomato, scallions, thyme, salt, peppercorns, and bay leaves.

MAKING VEGETABLE BROTH IN A PRESSURE COOKER

In addition to the basic vegetables used for making vegetable broth—onion, carrot, and celery—we found both cauliflower and tomato were also key. The cauliflower adds an important hearty, nutty flavor that forms the base flavor of the broth, while fresh tomato adds bright acidity along with a little color.

Since you are relying on humble vegetables (and some aromatics), it is important to eke as much flavor as possible out of them. Browning some in the pot before adding the liquid boosts the broth's flavor and color, while sautéing the garlic before adding the remaining ingredients mellows its harshness.

Adding a good dose of salt to the pot before cooking is very important when making vegetable broth. Not only does the salt season the broth as it cooks, but it also helps draw the moisture and flavor out of the vegetables and herbs.

Be careful not press on the solids when straining vegetable broth. If you press too hard, the softened vegetables will be forced through the strainer, which will make the broth cloudy and thick. Just let the solids sit in the strainer and drain naturally.

2. HIGH PRESSURE FOR 1 HOUR: Lock pressure-cooker lid in place and bring to high pressure over medium-high heat. As soon as pot reaches high pressure, reduce heat to medium-low and cook for 1 hour, adjusting heat as needed to maintain high pressure.

3. QUICK RELEASE PRESSURE: Remove pot from heat. Quick release pressure, then carefully remove lid, allowing steam to escape away from you.

4. Strain broth through fine-mesh strainer into clean container (do not press on solids); discard solids. (Broth can be refrigerated for up to 2 days, or frozen for several months.)

SOUPS, STEWS, AND CHILIS

Farmhouse Chicken Noodle Soup

✓ **WHY THIS RECIPE WORKS**

With its velvety broth and deep flavor, old-fashioned chicken noodle soup is an ideal pressure-cooker candidate since the pressure cooker can extract flavor from the meat, skin, and bones of a whole chicken in just 20 minutes. We started by putting the chicken into the pot with some aromatics, carrots, celery, and water. Placing the chicken in the pot breast side up allowed the thighs and more delicate breast meat to cook though at the same time since the thighs were in contact with the pot's bottom. After 20 minutes, the meat practically fell off the bones, making it easy to shred and stir back in. Soy sauce gave the broth even deeper, richer meaty flavor. To keep things simple, we cooked the noodles in the broth while we shredded the chicken.

INGREDIENTS

1   tablespoon vegetable oil
1   onion, chopped fine
3   garlic cloves, minced
1   teaspoon minced fresh thyme or ¼ teaspoon dried
8   cups water
4   carrots, peeled and sliced ½ inch thick
2   celery ribs, sliced ½ inch thick
2   tablespoons soy sauce
1   (4-pound) whole chicken, giblets discarded
    Salt and pepper
4   ounces (2⅔ cups) wide egg noodles
¼   cup minced fresh parsley

SERVES	TOTAL TIME
8	ABOUT 1 HOUR
PRESSURE LEVEL	RELEASE
HIGH	QUICK

20 MINUTES
UNDER PRESSURE

1. BUILD FLAVOR: Heat oil in pressure-cooker pot over medium heat until shimmering. Add onion and cook until softened, about 5 minutes. Stir in garlic and thyme and cook until fragrant, about 30 seconds. Stir in water, carrots, celery, and soy sauce, scraping up any browned bits. Season chicken with salt and pepper and place, breast side up, in pot.

2. HIGH PRESSURE FOR 20 MINUTES: Lock pressure-cooker lid in place and bring to high pressure over medium-high heat. As soon as pot reaches high pressure, reduce heat to medium-low and cook for 20 minutes, adjusting heat as needed to maintain high pressure.

3. QUICK RELEASE PRESSURE: Remove pot from heat. Quick release pressure, then carefully remove lid, allowing steam to escape away from you.

4. BEFORE SERVING: Transfer chicken to cutting board, let cool slightly, then shred meat into bite-size pieces, discarding skin and bones. Meanwhile, using large spoon, skim excess fat from surface of soup. Bring soup to boil, stir in noodles, and cook until tender, about 5 minutes. Stir in shredded chicken and parsley, season with salt and pepper to taste, and serve.

VARIATION

Farmhouse Chicken and Rice Soup
Substitute 1 cup long-grain white rice for egg noodles and cook until tender, 15 to 18 minutes.

MAKING CHICKEN NOODLE SOUP IN A PRESSURE COOKER

When cooking a whole chicken in the pressure cooker, we found it best to keep the delicate breast meat facing up to give it some protection from the direct heat and to promote even cooking.

Once cooked, the chicken will be very tender and nearly falling part. To remove the chicken from the pot for the shredding step, lift it out in one piece using tongs along with a large spoon for support.

The meat is easy to remove from the bones because it's so tender. Let the chicken cool slightly, then discard the skin and pull the meat off the bones. Shred the meat using two forks, gently pulling the meat apart and into bite-size strands.

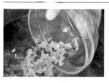
The last step is adding the noodles. Simmering them in the soup ensures they absorb flavor. Be sure to do this just before serving or else the noodles can become bloated and mushy.

TROUBLESHOOTING

Can I use a larger chicken?	It's not OK if you have a 6-quart pressure cooker; it just won't fit. However, if you have an 8-quart pressure cooker, you can use up to a 5-pound chicken and extend the pressurized cooking time to 30 minutes.
Can I substitute chicken parts for the whole chicken?	You can substitute an equal amount of bone-in thighs, and the cooking time will remain the same. You can also substitute bone-in chicken breasts. Because they're meatier, use 3 pounds rather than 4, and reduce the pressurized cooking time to 15 minutes.
What if I am not going to serve the soup right away?	Because the noodles will become mushy over time, it's best to add them to the soup and cook them just before serving.
Do I need to alter the recipe for a 6-quart electric pressure cooker?	Yes, quick release the pressure immediately after the pressurized cooking time; do not let the cooker switch to the warm setting. Use the browning (not the simmer) setting to cook the noodles in step 4.

Old-Fashioned Beef and Vegetable Soup

WHY THIS RECIPE WORKS

Beef and vegetable soup is a classic winter warmer-upper that typically requires a long simmer to tenderize a tough cut. We swapped in boneless beef short ribs for our usual chuck roast. Rich and well marbled, but without the intramuscular fat that has to be trimmed from a chuck roast, the short ribs were easy to cut up and could be perfectly cooked in 15 minutes. First, we browned all of the meat to maximize the beefy flavor, then we set it aside to sauté the onion, mushrooms, and thyme. Deglazing the pot with wine picked up the flavorful browned bits, while potatoes, carrots, and celery made our soup hearty. Look for boneless short ribs that are well marbled and measure about 2 inches wide and 1 inch thick.

INGREDIENTS

- 1 **pound boneless beef short ribs, trimmed and cut into ½-inch pieces**
  Salt and pepper
- 2 **tablespoons vegetable oil**
- 8 **ounces cremini mushrooms, trimmed and sliced ½ inch thick**
- 1 **onion, chopped fine**
- 2 **tablespoons tomato paste**
- 2 **teaspoons minced fresh thyme or ½ teaspoon dried**
- 1 **garlic clove, minced**
- 2 **tablespoons all-purpose flour**
- ¼ **cup dry red wine**
- 6 **cups beef broth**

SERVES	TOTAL TIME	
8	**ABOUT 1¼ HOURS**	**15 MINUTES**
PRESSURE LEVEL	RELEASE	
HIGH	**NATURAL**	**UNDER PRESSURE**

1 pound red potatoes, cut into
¾-inch pieces

3 carrots, peeled and cut into
½-inch pieces

2 celery ribs, cut into ½-inch
pieces

2 bay leaves

2 tablespoons minced fresh
parsley

1. BUILD FLAVOR: Pat beef dry with paper towels and season with salt and pepper. Heat 2 teaspoons oil in pressure-cooker pot over medium-high heat until just smoking. Brown half of meat on all sides, about 5 minutes; transfer to bowl. Repeat with 2 teaspoons oil and remaining beef.

2. Heat remaining 2 teaspoons oil in now-empty pot over medium heat until shimmering. Add mushrooms and onion and cook until softened, about 5 minutes. Stir in tomato paste, thyme, and garlic and cook until fragrant, about 30 seconds. Stir in flour and cook for 1 minute. Whisk in wine, scraping up any browned bits and smoothing out any lumps, and cook until slightly reduced, about 1 minute. Stir in broth, potatoes, carrots, celery, bay leaves, and beef with any accumulated juices.

3. HIGH PRESSURE FOR 15 MINUTES: Lock pressure-cooker lid in place and bring to high pressure over medium-high heat. As soon as pot reaches high pressure, reduce heat to medium-low and cook for 15 minutes, adjusting heat as needed to maintain high pressure.

MAKING BEEF AND VEGETABLE SOUP IN A PRESSURE COOKER

Cutting the beef to the right size is incredibly important, or else it will not cook at the same rate as the vegetables. Boneless short ribs are easy to cut into uniform pieces, just be sure to trim the fat off the meat or else your soup can turn out greasy.

Browning the meat ensures this beef soup is really beefy. Don't crowd the pan, and brown in batches for this step, to avoid steaming rather than searing the meat. The brown bits that form on the bottom of the pot (called fond) are as important for flavor as the browning of the meat.

TROUBLESHOOTING

Can I use bone-in short ribs instead of boneless?	Yes, but you will need to buy around 3 pounds to account for the bone, and you'll need to remove the bones to cut the meat up. The bones are packed with flavor, so add them to the pot with the broth and discard them with the bay leaves.
Can I use another cut of meat?	You can substitute 1 pound boneless beef chuck-eye roast, trimmed and cut into ½-inch pieces, in place of the boneless beef short ribs. The cooking time will remain the same.
Do I need to alter the recipe for a 6-quart electric pressure cooker?	Yes, turn the cooker off immediately after the pressurized cooking time and let the pressure release naturally for 15 minutes; do not let the cooker switch to the warm setting.

4. NATURALLY RELEASE PRESSURE: Remove pot from heat and allow pressure to release naturally for 15 minutes. Quick release any remaining pressure, then carefully remove lid, allowing steam to escape away from you.

5. BEFORE SERVING: Remove bay leaves. Using large spoon, skim excess fat from surface of soup. Stir in parsley, season with salt and pepper to taste, and serve.

VARIATION

Old-Fashioned Beef and Barley Soup
Omit potatoes. After removing bay leaves in step 5, stir in ½ cup pearl barley and simmer until tender, about 15 minutes, then continue as directed.

15-Bean Soup with Sausage

✓ WHY THIS RECIPE WORKS
We use store-bought 15-bean soup mix as the base for a quick homemade soup. Browning the sausage was a flavorful start, then we ditched the mix's flavoring packet in favor of carrot, onion, and aromatics. The pressure cooker tenderized the beans quickly, and salt-soaking them ensured even cooking. Smaller beans broke down and thickened the soup nicely. We cooked the sausages through whole to preserve their texture, then we sliced them and stirred them back in. Simmering the Swiss chard and tomato toward the end ensured gentle cooking. Garnish with Parmesan if desired.

INGREDIENTS

- 2 tablespoons vegetable oil
- 12 ounces hot or sweet Italian sausage
- 1 onion, chopped fine
- 1 carrot, peeled and chopped fine
- 4 garlic cloves, minced
- 1 teaspoon minced fresh thyme or ¼ teaspoon dried
- 4 cups low-sodium chicken broth
- 10 ounces (1½ cups) 15-bean soup mix, flavoring pack discarded, picked over, rinsed, and salt-soaked (see page 18)
- 2 bay leaves
- 8 ounces Swiss chard, stemmed and chopped
- 1 large tomato, cored and chopped
  Salt and pepper

SERVES	TOTAL TIME
4 TO 6	**ABOUT 1 HOUR***

PRESSURE LEVEL	RELEASE
HIGH	**QUICK**

*PLUS BEAN SOAKING TIME

25 MINUTES
UNDER PRESSURE

1. BUILD FLAVOR: Heat 1 tablespoon oil in pressure-cooker pot over medium-high heat until just smoking. Brown sausage on all sides, about 2 minutes; transfer to plate.

2. Heat remaining 1 tablespoon oil in now-empty pot over medium heat until shimmering. Add onion and carrot and cook until softened, about 5 minutes. Stir in garlic and thyme and cook until fragrant, about 30 seconds. Stir in broth, soaked beans, and bay leaves, scraping up any browned bits. Add sausage and any accumulated juices to pot.

3. HIGH PRESSURE FOR 25 MINUTES: Lock pressure-cooker lid in place and bring to high pressure over medium-high heat. As soon as pot reaches high pressure, reduce heat to medium-low and cook for 25 minutes, adjusting heat as needed to maintain high pressure.

4. QUICK RELEASE PRESSURE: Remove pot from heat. Quick release pressure, then carefully remove lid, allowing steam to escape away from you.

5. BEFORE SERVING: Remove bay leaves. Transfer sausage to cutting board and slice ½ inch thick. Meanwhile, bring soup to simmer, stir in chard and tomato, and cook until chard is tender, about 5 minutes. Stir in sliced sausage, season with salt and pepper to taste, and serve.

TEST KITCHEN TIP PREPARING SWISS CHARD

When cooking with greens like Swiss chard, collard greens, and kale, we often use only the leaves, and we add them to the pot to cook through briefly just before serving.

1. Cut away leafy green portion from either side of stem using chef's knife.

2. Stack several leaves on top of one another, and either slice leaves crosswise or chop into pieces (as specified in recipe). Wash and dry leaves after they are cut, using salad spinner.

TROUBLESHOOTING

Can I use other types of greens?
Other winter greens, such as collards and kale, can be substituted for the Swiss chard, but since they are tougher than chard, you will need to increase their simmering time. Simmer collards for about 15 minutes and kale for about 10 minutes. You can also add curly-leaf, flat-leaf, or baby spinach in place of the chard and simply stir it in until it is wilted, which happens quite quickly.

Can I double this recipe?
Not if you have a 6-quart pressure cooker; it just won't fit. However, if you have an 8-quart pressure cooker, you can double the recipe; the pressurized cooking time will remain the same.

Do I need to alter the recipe for a 6-quart electric pressure cooker?
Yes, quick release the pressure immediately after the pressurized cooking time; do not let the cooker switch to the warm setting. Use the browning (not the simmer) setting to simmer the soup in step 5.

Hearty Beef Stew

SERVES	TOTAL TIME
6	**ABOUT 1½ HOURS**

PRESSURE LEVEL	RELEASE
HIGH	**NATURAL**

25 MINUTES
UNDER PRESSURE

✓ WHY THIS RECIPE WORKS

To ensure a rich-tasting, company-worthy beef stew, we started with rich boneless beef short ribs. We found browning just half of the meat created plenty of flavorful fond in the pot and saved us time. We boosted the base of the stew by sautéing onions with a hefty amount of thyme and by adding tomato paste for sweetness and soy sauce for greater meaty depth. Red wine was the classic choice for deglazing the pot, and cooking it an extra minute before adding the remaining ingredients helped to mellow its sharpness. To keep the potatoes and carrots tender but distinct while cooking under pressure, cutting them into large 1-inch pieces proved key. Peas are a classic addition to beef stew; we waited to add them until the very end, since they only needed to warm through. Look for boneless short ribs that are well marbled and measure about 2 inches wide and 1 inch thick.

INGREDIENTS

- 3 **pounds boneless beef short ribs, trimmed and cut into 1-inch pieces**
  Salt and pepper
- 2 **tablespoons vegetable oil**
- 2 **onions, chopped**
- 2 **tablespoons tomato paste**
- 1 **tablespoon minced fresh thyme or 1 teaspoon dried**
- ⅓ **cup all-purpose flour**
- 1 **cup dry red wine**
- 2 **cups beef broth**

1½ **pounds red potatoes, cut into
   1-inch pieces**
1 **pound carrots, peeled and
   sliced 1 inch thick**
¼ **cup soy sauce**
2 **bay leaves**
1½ **cups frozen peas**
¼ **cup minced fresh parsley**

1. BUILD FLAVOR: Pat beef dry with paper towels and season with salt and pepper. Heat 1 tablespoon oil in pressure-cooker pot over medium-high heat until just smoking. Brown half of meat on all sides, about 8 minutes; transfer to bowl.

2. Heat remaining 1 tablespoon oil in now-empty pot over medium heat until shimmering. Add onions and cook until softened, about 5 minutes. Stir in tomato paste and thyme and cook until fragrant, about 30 seconds. Stir in flour and cook for 1 minute. Whisk in wine, scraping up any browned bits and smoothing out any lumps, and cook until slightly reduced, about 1 minute. Stir in broth, potatoes, carrots, soy sauce, bay leaves, browned beef with any accumulated juices, and remaining beef.

3. HIGH PRESSURE FOR 25 MINUTES: Lock pressure-cooker lid in place and bring to high pressure over medium-high heat. As soon as pot reaches high pressure, reduce heat to medium-low and cook for 25 minutes, adjusting heat as needed to maintain high pressure.

MAKING BEEF STEW IN A PRESSURE COOKER

For big beefy flavor and a meltingly tender texture, cuts from the shoulder and boneless short ribs could both work since they have plenty of intramuscular fat and collagen to keep the meat moist. We use short ribs here since they are easy to cut into even-size pieces.

Getting the doneness of the potatoes and carrots just right took some testing. To get them to cook at the same rate as the beef and not disintegrate under pressure, we found both vegetables had to be cut into large 1-inch pieces.

For a properly thick stew, we add flour after browning the meat and onions. This allows the flour to mix with the fat in the pot (creating a roux of sorts) and keeps it from clumping. Be sure to incorporate the flour completely before adding the broth.

Even if you trim the short ribs really well before cooking, there will be some fat on the surface of the stew after you remove the lid. Use a large, wide spoon to skim this excess fat away before serving.

TROUBLESHOOTING

Can I double this recipe?

No. This recipe makes 14 cups of stew, so whether you are using a 6-quart or an 8-quart pot, a double-batch would overfill the capacity.

Do I need to alter the recipe for a 6-quart electric pressure cooker?

Yes, turn the cooker off immediately after the pressurized cooking time and let the pressure release naturally for 15 minutes; do not let the cooker switch to the warm setting.

4. NATURALLY RELEASE PRESSURE: Remove pot from heat and allow pressure to release naturally for 15 minutes. Quick release any remaining pressure, then carefully remove lid, allowing steam to escape away from you.

5. BEFORE SERVING: Remove bay leaves. Using large spoon, skim excess fat from surface of stew. Stir in peas and let stand for 5 minutes. Stir in parsley, season with salt and pepper to taste, and serve.

Chipotle Pork and Hominy Stew

WHY THIS RECIPE WORKS

The Mexican stew posole is all about the combination of hominy, spice, and tender chunks of pork. With the help of the pressure cooker, the pork turns ultratender and is infused with the heady flavor of the stew in no time. Plenty of onion plus jalapeños and garlic ensured the right bold hit, while chipotle chiles brought smoky depth and spice. We used canned hominy since it's widely available and could be stirred in at the end of cooking just to heat through. A final addition of minced cilantro added brightness and the right touch of flavor. Pork butt roast is often labeled Boston butt in the supermarket. Serve with diced tomato, diced avocado, minced jalapeño, and crunchy garnishes like thinly sliced radishes and green cabbage.

INGREDIENTS

- 3 **pounds boneless pork butt roast, trimmed and cut into 1-inch pieces**
  Salt and pepper
- 2 **tablespoons vegetable oil**
- 2 **onions, chopped**
- 2 **jalapeño chiles, stemmed, seeded, and minced**
- 4 **garlic cloves, minced**
- 1 **tablespoon minced canned chipotle chile in adobo sauce**
- 2 **teaspoons minced fresh oregano or ½ teaspoon dried**
- ⅓ **cup all-purpose flour**
- 1 **cup dry white wine**
- 3 **cups low-sodium chicken broth**

SERVES	TOTAL TIME	
6	**ABOUT 1½ HOURS**	**30**
PRESSURE LEVEL	RELEASE	**MINUTES**
HIGH	**NATURAL**	**UNDER PRESSURE**

1 **pound carrots, peeled and sliced 1 inch thick**

2 **bay leaves**

2 **(15-ounce) cans white or yellow hominy, rinsed**

¼ **cup minced fresh cilantro**

1. BUILD FLAVOR: Pat pork dry with paper towels and season with salt and pepper. Heat 1 tablespoon oil in pressure-cooker pot over medium-high heat until just smoking. Brown half of meat on all sides, about 8 minutes; transfer to bowl.

2. Heat remaining 1 tablespoon oil in now-empty pot over medium heat until shimmering. Add onions and cook until softened, about 5 minutes. Stir in jalapeños, garlic, chipotle, and oregano and cook until fragrant, about 30 seconds. Stir in flour and cook for 1 minute. Whisk in wine, scraping up any browned bits and smoothing out any lumps, and cook until slightly reduced, about 1 minute. Stir in broth, carrots, bay leaves, browned pork with any accumulated juices, and remaining pork.

3. HIGH PRESSURE FOR 30 MINUTES: Lock pressure-cooker lid in place and bring to high pressure over medium-high heat. As soon as pot reaches high pressure, reduce heat to medium-low and cook for 30 minutes, adjusting heat as needed to maintain high pressure.

TEST KITCHEN TIP CUTTING PORK BUTT FOR STEW

Pork butt is made up of several different muscles held together with fat and sinew. When cutting it into pieces for stew meat, you will need to use your hands as well as a sharp knife.

1. Pull roast apart at major seams (delineated by lines of fat and silverskin), using sharp knife if necessary.

2. Trim off excess fat and silverskin, then cut meat into 1-inch chunks.

TROUBLESHOOTING

Can I substitute a different cut of pork?	Yes, we recommend boneless country-style pork ribs (use an equal amount) because they're similarly fatty and will therefore stay moist, tender, and juicy. Avoid a lean cut like pork loin, which would turn out dry.
Can I make this stew spicier?	Yes, you can either reserve the jalapeño seeds and add them to the pot with the jalapeños, or increase the chipotle chiles.
Do I need to alter the recipe for a 6-quart electric pressure cooker?	Yes, turn the cooker off immediately after the pressurized cooking time and let the pressure release naturally for 15 minutes; do not let the cooker switch to the warm setting. Use the browning (not the simmer) setting to simmer the stew in step 5.

4. NATURALLY RELEASE PRESSURE: Remove pot from heat and allow pressure to release naturally for 15 minutes. Quick release any remaining pressure, then carefully remove lid, allowing steam to escape away from you.

5. BEFORE SERVING: Remove bay leaves. Using large spoon, skim excess fat from surface of stew. Bring stew to simmer, stir in hominy, and cook until heated through, about 5 minutes. Stir in cilantro, season with salt and pepper to taste, and serve.

Rustic French Pork and White Bean Stew

WHY THIS RECIPE WORKS

This French-inspired dish, with chunks of pork, creamy white beans, fennel, and carrots, tastes like it simmered all day, yet the pressure cooker makes it doable on a weeknight—even with dried beans in the mix. To keep the cooking time down, we browned only half the meat and still built enough flavorful fond on the bottom of the pot to season the stew. We continued to build a base with sautéed onion, garlic, and herbes de Provence before deglazing the pot with white wine. To ensure each component cooked through evenly, we cut the carrots and fennel into large 1-inch pieces and salt-soaked the beans. Once everything was tender, parsley and lemon juice went in to brighten the flavors. Pork butt roast is often labeled Boston butt in the supermarket.

INGREDIENTS

- 3 pounds boneless pork butt roast, trimmed and cut into 1-inch pieces (see page 35)
  Salt and pepper
- 2 tablespoons vegetable oil
- 2 onions, chopped
- 8 garlic cloves, minced
- 1½ teaspoons herbes de Provence
- ⅓ cup all-purpose flour
- 1 cup dry white wine
- 3 cups low-sodium chicken broth
- 1 pound carrots, peeled and sliced 1 inch thick
- 1 fennel bulb, stalks discarded, bulb halved, cored, and cut into 1-inch pieces

SERVES	TOTAL TIME
6	ABOUT 1½ HOURS*

PRESSURE LEVEL	RELEASE
HIGH	NATURAL

30 MINUTES
UNDER PRESSURE

*PLUS BEAN SOAKING TIME

8   ounces (1¼ cups) dried
    cannellini beans, picked over,
    rinsed, and salt-soaked
    (see page 18)
2   bay leaves
¼   cup minced fresh parsley
1   tablespoon lemon juice,
    plus extra as needed

1. BUILD FLAVOR: Pat pork dry with paper towels and season with salt and pepper. Heat 1 tablespoon oil in pressure-cooker pot over medium-high heat until just smoking. Brown half of meat on all sides, about 8 minutes; transfer to bowl.

2. Heat remaining 1 tablespoon oil in now-empty pot over medium heat until shimmering. Add onions and cook until softened, about 5 minutes. Stir in garlic and herbes de Provence and cook until fragrant, about 30 seconds. Stir in flour and cook for 1 minute. Whisk in wine, scraping up any browned bits and smoothing out any lumps, and cook until slightly reduced, about 1 minute. Stir in broth, carrots, fennel, soaked beans, bay leaves, browned pork with any accumulated juices, and remaining pork.

3. HIGH PRESSURE FOR 30 MINUTES: Lock pressure-cooker lid in place and bring to high pressure over medium-high heat. As soon as pot reaches high pressure, reduce heat to medium-low and cook for 30 minutes, adjusting heat as needed to maintain high pressure.

TEST KITCHEN TIP PREPPING FENNEL

1. After cutting off stalks and feathery fronds, cut thin slice from base of bulb and remove any tough or blemished outer layers.

2. Cut bulb in half vertically through base, then use small knife to remove pyramid-shaped core. Continue to cut halves into pieces as directed in recipe.

TROUBLESHOOTING

Can I substitute canned beans for the dried?	Yes, although the final stew will not be as thick since the dried beans soak up some of the liquid, and we also found the flavor wasn't as developed. Before adding the parsley and lemon juice in step 5, stir 2 (15-ounce) cans of rinsed cannellini beans into the stew and simmer until the beans are heated through, about 5 minutes.
Can I use chicken instead of pork?	Boneless chicken thighs would work fine, although we found they release more juices than the pork and thus create a looser stew. Substitute an equal amount of boneless thighs, cut into 1-inch pieces, for the pork butt and reduce the pressurized cooking time to 20 minutes.
Do I need to alter the recipe for a 6-quart electric pressure cooker?	Yes, turn the cooker off immediately after the pressurized cooking time and let the pressure release naturally for 15 minutes; do not let the cooker switch to the warm setting.

4. NATURALLY RELEASE PRESSURE: Remove pot from heat and allow pressure to release naturally for 15 minutes. Quick release any remaining pressure, then carefully remove lid, allowing steam to escape away from you.

5. BEFORE SERVING: Remove bay leaves. Using large spoon, skim excess fat from surface of stew. Stir in parsley and lemon juice and season with salt, pepper, and extra lemon juice to taste. Serve.

Pork Vindaloo

✓ **WHY THIS RECIPE WORKS**

This classic Indian dish with chunks of pork gently and slowly simmered in a rich, warmly spiced tomato sauce becomes a weeknight option with the help of the pressure cooker. As with our other pressure-cooker pork stews, we chose boneless pork butt for our vindaloo since it has enough fat to keep the meat tender and juicy during cooking. A hefty amount of spice is key in this dish, but using too much produced a chalky texture. We found that blooming a moderate amount of mustard seeds, paprika, cumin, cayenne, and cloves in oil with our aromatics allowed us to maximize each spice's flavor and aroma while avoiding grittiness in the final dish. Some sugar and red wine vinegar, stirred in with the tomatoes before adding the pork and locking on the lid, balanced the flavors. Pork butt roast is often labeled Boston butt in the supermarket.

INGREDIENTS

- 3 **pounds boneless pork butt roast, trimmed and cut into 1-inch pieces (see page 35)**
  Salt and pepper
- 2 **tablespoons vegetable oil**
- 3 **onions, chopped fine**
- 8 **garlic cloves, minced**
- 1 **tablespoon mustard seeds**
- 1 **tablespoon paprika**
- 1 **teaspoon ground cumin**
- ¼ **teaspoon cayenne pepper**
- ⅛ **teaspoon ground cloves**
- ¼ **cup all-purpose flour**

SERVES	TOTAL TIME
6	**ABOUT 1½ HOURS**

PRESSURE LEVEL	RELEASE
HIGH	**NATURAL**

30 MINUTES
UNDER PRESSURE

1 **cup low-sodium chicken broth**
1 **(14.5-ounce) can diced tomatoes**
2 **tablespoons red wine vinegar**
1 **teaspoon sugar**
¼ **cup minced fresh cilantro**

1. BUILD FLAVOR: Pat pork dry with paper towels and season with salt and pepper. Heat 1 tablespoon oil in pressure-cooker pot over medium-high heat until just smoking. Brown half of meat on all sides, about 8 minutes; transfer to bowl.

2. Heat remaining 1 tablespoon oil in now-empty pot over medium heat until shimmering. Add onions and ¼ teaspoon salt and cook until softened, about 5 minutes. Stir in garlic, mustard seeds, paprika, cumin, cayenne, and cloves and cook just until fragrant, about 30 seconds. Stir in flour and cook for 1 minute. Whisk in broth, scraping up any browned bits and smoothing out any lumps. Stir in tomatoes, vinegar, sugar, browned pork with any accumulated juices, and remaining pork.

3. HIGH PRESSURE FOR 30 MINUTES: Lock pressure-cooker lid in place and bring to high pressure over medium-high heat. As soon as pot reaches high pressure, reduce heat to medium-low and cook for 30 minutes, adjusting heat as needed to maintain high pressure.

TEST KITCHEN TIP BLOOMING DRIED SPICES

Because the aroma and flavor compounds in spices are primarily oil soluble rather than water soluble, we often "bloom" them by cooking them in oil.

Once onions have been cooked, add spices (and garlic) to pot and cook just until fragrant, about 30 seconds.

TROUBLESHOOTING

Can I use another cut of meat?	Lamb is a classic choice for vindaloo. Substitute 3 pounds leg of lamb, trimmed and cut into 1-inch pieces, for the pork butt; the pressurized cooking time will remain the same. You can also substitute 3 pounds boneless chicken thighs, cut into 1-inch pieces; reduce the pressurized cooking time to 20 minutes and use a quick release rather than a natural.
Can I substitute another spice for the cloves?	Another warm spice, such as cinnamon, nutmeg, or mace, would work.
Do I need to alter the recipe for a 6-quart electric pressure cooker?	Yes, increase the amount of chicken broth to 2 cups. Turn the cooker off immediately after the pressurized cooking time and let the pressure release naturally for 15 minutes; do not let the cooker switch to the warm setting. Before serving, simmer the stew for 15 minutes to thicken using the browning (not the simmer) setting.

4. NATURALLY RELEASE PRESSURE: Remove pot from heat and allow pressure to release naturally for 15 minutes. Quick release any remaining pressure, then carefully remove lid, allowing steam to escape away from you.

5. BEFORE SERVING: Using large spoon, skim excess fat from surface of soup. Stir in cilantro, season with salt and pepper to taste, and serve.

Chickpea and Artichoke Tagine

SERVES
4 TO 6

TOTAL TIME
ABOUT 1 HOUR*

PRESSURE LEVEL
HIGH

RELEASE
QUICK

*PLUS BEAN SOAKING TIME

25 MINUTES
UNDER PRESSURE

✓ WHY THIS RECIPE WORKS

This Moroccan-style vegetarian stew gets complex flavor from a blend of warm spices, onions, garlic, and lemon zest. Turning to the pressure cooker meant we could enjoy the flavor and texture of dried chickpeas rather than canned. Since delicate vegetables can easily overcook in the pressure cooker, we opted to stir in our artichokes hearts (which we browned first to remove their raw flavor) once the chickpeas had finished cooking. Chopped kalamata olives rounded out the Mediterranean profile, fresh cilantro lent brightness, and a drizzle of olive oil gave it the right rich finish.

INGREDIENTS

- 2 tablespoons extra-virgin olive oil, plus extra for serving
- 1 onion, halved and sliced thin
- 4 (2-inch) strips lemon zest
- 6 garlic cloves, minced
- 1 tablespoon paprika
- ½ teaspoon ground cumin
- ¼ teaspoon ground cinnamon
- ⅛ teaspoon cayenne pepper
- 2 tablespoons all-purpose flour
- 3 cups vegetable broth
- 1 pound carrots, peeled and sliced ½ inch thick
- 1 (15-ounce) can diced tomatoes
- 8 ounces (1¼ cups) dried chickpeas, picked over, rinsed, and salt-soaked (see page 18)
- 9 ounces frozen artichoke hearts, thawed and patted dry

½ **cup pitted kalamata olives, halved**
½ **cup minced fresh cilantro**
   Salt and pepper

1. BUILD FLAVOR: Heat 1 tablespoon oil in pressure-cooker pot over medium heat until shimmering. Add onion and cook until softened, about 5 minutes. Stir in lemon zest, garlic, paprika, cumin, cinnamon, and cayenne and cook until fragrant, about 30 seconds. Stir in flour and cook for 1 minute. Whisk in broth, scraping up any browned bits and smoothing out any lumps. Stir in carrots, tomatoes, and chickpeas.

2. HIGH PRESSURE FOR 25 MINUTES: Lock pressure-cooker lid in place and bring to high pressure over medium-high heat. As soon as pot reaches high pressure, reduce heat to medium-low heat and cook for 25 minutes, adjusting heat as needed to maintain high pressure.

3. QUICK RELEASE PRESSURE: Remove pot from heat. Quick release pressure, then carefully remove lid, allowing steam to escape away from you.

4. BEFORE SERVING: Heat remaining 1 tablespoon oil in 12-inch skillet over medium heat until shimmering. Add artichokes and cook until golden brown, 5 to 7 minutes. Remove lemon zest from stew. Stir in artichokes, olives, and cilantro and season with salt and pepper to taste. Drizzle individual portions with oil before serving.

MAKING CHICKPEA TAGINE IN A PRESSURE COOKER

Soaking chickpeas in salt water the day before cooking them ensures they cook through evenly and makes them less likely to burst open. Soaking also gives their skins a softer texture.

Before adding the soaked beans to the pot, we build flavor by sautéing onion, garlic, a few spices, and lemon zest. Use a vegetable peeler to remove the zest from the lemon in strips, avoiding the bitter white pith underneath. The zest perfumes the dish and can be easily removed before serving.

Since artichokes are delicate, we stir them in after cooking the chickpeas under pressure. To help bring out their flavor, we brown them first. Frozen artichokes brown more easily than canned because they are less waterlogged. For efficiency, brown the artichokes while the stew cooks.

TROUBLESHOOTING

Can I substitute water or another broth for the vegetable broth?	To keep things vegetarian, substitute 3 cups water for the broth and add 2 teaspoons tomato paste and 2 teaspoons soy sauce to the pot with the water. If you're not a vegetarian, you can substitute 3 cups low-sodium chicken broth.
Do I need to alter the recipe for a 6-quart electric pressure cooker?	Yes, quick release the pressure immediately after the pressurized cooking time; do not let the cooker switch to the warm setting.

VARIATIONS

Chickpea Tagine with Dried Apricots and Honey
Omit artichokes and substitute ½ cup pitted and halved green olives for kalamata olives. Add 1 cup dried chopped apricots and 2 tablespoons honey with olives.

Chickpea Tagine with Cauliflower and Almonds
Omit artichokes. Add ½ head cauliflower, cored and cut into 1-inch florets, to finished tagine and simmer until tender, 10 to 12 minutes. Stir in ¼ cup chopped, toasted almonds before serving.

1/29/16
Very good
and easy
- only used 1 TBP of chili
powder
- made w/ cornbread

Easy Weeknight Chili

SERVES	TOTAL TIME
4 TO 6	**ABOUT 45 MINUTES**

PRESSURE LEVEL	RELEASE
HIGH	**QUICK**

10 MINUTES
UNDER PRESSURE

✔ WHY THIS RECIPE WORKS

Getting a ground beef chili with bold, long-simmered flavor in a pressure cooker is easy because under pressure the meat quickly picks up the flavor of the spices. A combination of chili powder, cumin, and garlic was all it took to get the job done. We used crushed tomatoes plus chicken broth for a base with the proper consistency. Browning the beef to develop flavor is standard in most ground beef chilis, but we found browned meat overcooked and became gritty in the pressure cooker. To avoid this, we cooked the meat until it just lost its pink color. Given the 10-minute cooking time, dried beans weren't an option, so we turned to canned kidney beans. Serve with your favorite chili garnishes.

INGREDIENTS

- 2 **tablespoons vegetable oil**
- 1 **onion, chopped fine**
- 2 **tablespoons chili powder**
- 2 **teaspoons ground cumin**
- 4 **garlic cloves, minced**
  Salt and pepper
- 1 **pound 85 percent lean ground beef**
- 1 **(28-ounce) can crushed tomatoes**
- 1 **cup low-sodium chicken broth**
- 2 **(15-ounce) cans kidney beans, rinsed**

1. BUILD FLAVOR: Heat oil in pressure-cooker pot over medium heat until shimmering. Add onion and cook until softened, about 5 minutes. Stir in chili powder, cumin, garlic, and ½ teaspoon salt and cook until fragrant, about 1 minute. Add beef and cook, breaking up meat with wooden spoon, until no longer pink, about 4 minutes. Stir in tomatoes and broth, scraping up any browned bits.

2. HIGH PRESSURE FOR 10 MINUTES: Lock pressure-cooker lid in place and bring to high pressure over medium-high heat. As soon as pot reaches high pressure, reduce heat to medium-low and cook for 10 minutes, adjusting heat as needed to maintain high pressure.

3. QUICK RELEASE PRESSURE: Remove pot from heat. Quick release pressure, then carefully remove lid, allowing steam to escape away from you.

4. BEFORE SERVING: Bring chili to simmer, stir in beans, and cook until heated through, about 5 minutes. Season with salt and pepper to taste and serve.

VARIATION

Easy Weeknight Chili with Moroccan Spices and Chickpeas
Omit chili powder. Add 4 teaspoons sweet paprika, 1 tablespoon ground ginger, and ½ teaspoon ground cinnamon to pot with cumin, garlic, and salt. Substitute 2 (15-ounce) cans chickpeas, rinsed, for kidney beans. Add 1 cup raisins, if desired, to pot with the beans before serving.

MAKING WEEKNIGHT CHILI IN A PRESSURE COOKER

The first key to making a great chili is to bring out the flavors and mellow the raw edge of the spices that go into it by sautéing (or blooming) them quickly in oil before adding the meat, tomatoes, and liquids.

Using 85 percent lean ground beef is important. Anything fattier and your chili will be greasy; anything leaner and the meat will taste dry and tough. We stir the beef into the bloomed spices to infuse the meat with flavor.

For the right sauciness, we found a combination of crushed tomatoes and broth works best. Unlike diced tomatoes, which won't break down, or tomato puree, which tastes overly sweet in this scenario, crushed tomatoes have a smooth texture and fresh flavor that work well here.

Since this chili needs only 10 minutes under pressure, dried beans aren't an option. So we add canned beans and simmer the chili just until they are heated through but not long enough that they start to break down. Be sure to drain and rinse the canned beans before adding them to the pot.

TROUBLESHOOTING

Can I use ground turkey instead of ground beef?	Yes, but make sure to buy 93 percent lean ground turkey, not ground turkey breast (also labeled 99 percent fat free), or else the meat will taste very dry.
Can I double this recipe?	Yes, double the amount of each ingredient and increase the simmering time in step 4 to 15 minutes.
Can I make this chili spicier?	Yes, add ½ teaspoon cayenne pepper along with the other spices to the pot in step 1.
Do I need to alter the recipe for a 6-quart electric pressure cooker?	Yes, quick release the pressure immediately after the pressurized cooking time; do not let the cooker switch to the warm setting. Increase the chili simmering time to 15 minutes in step 4, and use the browning (not the simmer) setting.

Texas-Style Chili con Carne

WHY THIS RECIPE WORKS

Texans are famous for their style of chili featuring chunks of beef in a chile-infused sauce. Boneless short ribs turned tender in under 30 minutes. To thicken our base of chicken broth and crushed tomatoes, we experimented with ingredients like flour and cornstarch, but we settled on corn tortillas. Grinding them in the food processor ensured they melted into the chili, thickening it up and giving it a subtle corn flavor. Traditional recipes call for dried chiles, but we found the pressure cooker did a great job of intensifying basic pantry spices. Serve with your favorite chili garnishes.

INGREDIENTS

6 (6-inch) corn tortillas, chopped coarse
5 pounds boneless beef short ribs, trimmed and cut into 1-inch chunks
   Salt and pepper
3 tablespoons vegetable oil
1 onion, chopped
3 tablespoons chili powder
2 tablespoons ground cumin
5 garlic cloves, minced
4 teaspoons minced canned chipotle chile in adobo sauce
3 cups low-sodium chicken broth
1 (28-ounce) can crushed tomatoes
8 ounces (1¼ cups) dried kidney beans, picked over, rinsed, and salt-soaked (see page 18)
2 tablespoons soy sauce

SERVES	TOTAL TIME
6 TO 8	**ABOUT 1¼ HOURS***

PRESSURE LEVEL	RELEASE
HIGH	**NATURAL**

*PLUS BEAN SOAKING TIME

25 MINUTES
UNDER PRESSURE

1. BUILD FLAVOR: Process tortilla pieces in food processor to fine crumbs, about 30 seconds; set aside. Pat beef dry with paper towels and season with salt and pepper. Heat 1 tablespoon oil in pressure-cooker pot over medium-high heat until just smoking. Brown one-quarter meat on all sides, about 8 minutes; transfer to bowl. Repeat with 1 tablespoon oil and one-quarter meat.

2. Heat remaining 1 tablespoon oil in now-empty pot over medium heat until shimmering. Add onion and cook until softened, about 5 minutes. Stir in chili powder, cumin, garlic, and chipotle and cook until fragrant, about 30 seconds. Stir in broth, scraping up any browned bits. Stir in tomatoes, soaked beans, soy sauce, browned beef with any accumulated juices, and remaining beef. Sprinkle processed tortillas over top.

3. HIGH PRESSURE FOR 25 MINUTES: Lock pressure-cooker lid in place and bring to high pressure over medium-high heat. As soon as pot reaches high pressure, reduce heat to medium-low and cook for 25 minutes, adjusting heat as needed to maintain high pressure.

4. NATURALLY RELEASE PRESSURE: Remove pot from heat and allow pressure to release naturally for 15 minutes. Quick release any remaining pressure, then carefully remove lid, allowing steam to escape away from you. Serve.

MAKING TEXAS-STYLE CHILI IN A PRESSURE COOKER

To thicken this chili, corn tortillas are perfect for the job. They not only add an authentic flavor of corn masa (a traditional addition to Texas chili), but are easy to find. To ensure they break down during cooking, we process them into crumbs in the food processor first.

Texas chili consists of tender chunks of beef, rather than ground beef like most chilis, and we quickly settled on using boneless short ribs. Not only are they easy to cut up into uniform pieces for even cooking, but they also turn meltingly tender and stay moist as they cook.

Many recipes for this style of chili call for whole dried chiles, which require toasting and soaking. We can skip that complicated route since the pressure cooker naturally intensifies simple spices. Chili powder, cumin, garlic, and chipotle gave us a chili with deep, heady flavor and aroma.

Unlike ground meat chili that cooks for only 10 minutes, Texas chili requires a longer cooking time (much like a stew), so using dried beans here makes sense. Be sure to salt-soak the beans before cooking or else they will not cook at the same rate as the beef and will not hold their shape.

TROUBLESHOOTING

Do I need to alter the recipe for a 6-quart stovetop or an electric pressure cooker?

Only half of the recipe will fit in a 6-quart pot. Reduce all ingredients by half; the pressurized cooking time will stay the same. For an electric cooker, turn the cooker off immediately after the pressurized cooking time and let the pressure release naturally for 15 minutes; do not let the cooker switch to the warm setting.

VARIATIONS
Fiery Texas-Style Chili con Carne

Substitute 1 (28-ounce) can fire-roasted crushed tomatoes for crushed tomatoes and add 2 stemmed, seeded, and minced jalapeño chiles and 1 teaspoon cayenne with chili powder.

Sweet and Smoky Texas-Style Chili con Carne

Add ¼ cup dark brown sugar and ½ teaspoon liquid smoke with tomatoes. Reduce chipotle to 1 tablespoon.

Mole Chicken Chili

WHY THIS RECIPE WORKS

In Mexico, slowly simmered mole—a rich, complex sauce typically made with onions, garlic, dried chiles, chocolate, nuts, and spices—is often paired with chicken. We decided to translate the idea into a pressure-cooker shredded chicken chili. Traditional mole relies on a long ingredient list, but we simply fine-tuned a mix of pantry staples like chili powder, cocoa, cinnamon, cloves, raisins, and peanut butter, until it had just the right profile. After simmering the mixture to let the flavors meld, we pureed it in the blender for a smooth sauce. Back in the pot and under pressure, our mole infused the chicken with bold flavor. Red bell pepper added sweetness, texture, and color, while the mild acidity of diced tomatoes balanced the richness, and cilantro brightened it up. Garnish with peanuts, onion, tomatoes, and cilantro, if desired.

INGREDIENTS

3	tablespoons vegetable oil
2	tablespoons chili powder
2	tablespoons cocoa
3	garlic cloves, minced
2	teaspoons minced canned chipotle chile in adobo sauce
½	teaspoon ground cinnamon
⅛	teaspoon ground cloves
2½	cups low-sodium chicken broth
1	(14.5-ounce) can diced tomatoes
1	cup raisins
¼	cup peanut butter

SERVES	TOTAL TIME
4 TO 6	**ABOUT 1¼ HOURS**

PRESSURE LEVEL	RELEASE
HIGH	**QUICK**

25 MINUTES

UNDER PRESSURE

4	**pounds bone-in chicken thighs, skin removed, trimmed**
	Salt and pepper
1	**onion, halved and sliced ½ inch thick**
1	**red bell pepper, stemmed, seeded, and cut into ½-inch pieces**
¼	**cup minced fresh cilantro**

1. BUILD FLAVOR: Heat 2 tablespoons oil in pressure-cooker pot over medium heat until shimmering. Add chili powder, cocoa, garlic, chipotle, cinnamon, and cloves and cook until fragrant, about 30 seconds. Stir in broth, tomatoes, raisins, and peanut butter, scraping up any browned bits. Bring to simmer and cook for 5 minutes. Puree sauce in blender until smooth, about 30 seconds.

2. Season chicken with salt and pepper. Heat remaining 1 tablespoon oil in now-empty pot. Add onion and cook until softened, about 5 minutes. Stir in sauce, then add chicken to pot.

3. HIGH PRESSURE FOR 25 MINUTES: Lock pressure-cooker lid in place and bring to high pressure over medium-high heat. As soon as pot reaches high pressure, reduce heat to medium-low and cook for 25 minutes, adjusting heat as needed to maintain high pressure.

4. QUICK RELEASE PRESSURE: Remove pot from heat. Quick release pressure, then carefully remove lid, allowing steam to escape away from you.

TEST KITCHEN TIP CUTTING UP A BELL PEPPER

We've found that the most efficient way to handle this awkwardly shaped vegetable is to slice off the top and bottom, then cut the body of the pepper in one place so that it can be opened up and lay flat on the cutting board.

1. Slice off top and bottom of pepper and remove seeds and stem. Slice down through side of pepper.

2. Lay pepper flat on cutting board, trim away any remaining ribs and seeds, then cut into pieces or strips as desired.

TROUBLESHOOTING

| **Can I substitute chicken breasts in this recipe?** | We wouldn't recommend it if you are after chili with the same texture and consistency as our master recipe since breasts shred into thinner strands and soak up more sauce. However, we did think that this recipe made with an equal amount of bone-in breasts made a fantastic filling for tacos or burritos. Reduce the pressurized cooking time to 15 minutes. |
| **Do I need to alter the recipe for a 6-quart electric pressure cooker?** | Yes, quick release the pressure immediately after the pressurized cooking time; do not let the cooker switch to the warm setting. Use the browning (not the simmer) setting to simmer the chili in step 5. |

5. BEFORE SERVING: Transfer chicken to cutting board, let cool slightly, then shred meat into bite-size pieces, discarding skin and bones. Meanwhile, bring chili to simmer, stir in bell pepper, and cook until tender, 10 to 15 minutes. Stir in shredded chicken and cilantro, season with salt and pepper to taste, and serve.

Vegetarian Black Bean Chili

SERVES	TOTAL TIME
4 TO 6	**ABOUT 1½ HOURS**

PRESSURE LEVEL	RELEASE
HIGH	**QUICK**

45 MINUTES
UNDER PRESSURE

✔ WHY THIS RECIPE WORKS

Vegetarian black bean chili is tricky since you can't use the smoky ham hock or bacon that you typically find in non-vegetarian versions. For flavor without the meat, we browned a good amount of aromatics and spices and made sure to use flavorful dried beans rather than canned. The pressure cooker cut their traditional cooking time in half. Soaking dried beans helps prevent them from bursting, but here we opted to just rinse them since broken beans helped thicken the chili. Serve with your favorite chili garnishes.

INGREDIENTS

3   tablespoons vegetable oil
1   onion, chopped
3   tablespoons chili powder
2   tablespoons ground cumin
9   garlic cloves, minced
1–3   teaspoons minced canned chipotle chile in adobo sauce
2½   cups vegetable broth
2½   cups water
1   (28-ounce) can crushed tomatoes
1   pound (2½ cups) dried black beans, picked over and rinsed
1   pound white mushrooms, trimmed and quartered
2   bay leaves
2   red bell peppers, stemmed, seeded, and cut into ½-inch pieces
½   cup minced fresh cilantro
   Salt and pepper

1. BUILD FLAVOR: Heat oil in pressure-cooker pot over medium heat until shimmering. Add onion and cook until softened, about 5 minutes. Stir in chili powder, cumin, garlic, and chipotle and cook until fragrant, about 30 seconds. Stir in broth, water, tomatoes, beans, mushrooms, and bay leaves, scraping up any browned bits.

2. HIGH PRESSURE FOR 45 MINUTES: Lock pressure-cooker lid in place and bring to high pressure over medium-high heat. As soon as pot reaches high pressure, reduce heat to medium-low and cook for 45 minutes, adjusting heat as needed to maintain high pressure.

3. QUICK RELEASE PRESSURE: Remove pot from heat. Quick release pressure, then carefully remove lid, allowing steam to escape away from you.

4. BEFORE SERVING: Remove bay leaves. Bring chili to simmer, stir in bell peppers, and cook until tender, 10 to 15 minutes. Stir in cilantro, season with salt and pepper to taste, and serve.

VARIATIONS

Tequila and Lime Black Bean Chili
Stir 3 tablespoons tequila into pot with broth. Stir 1 tablespoon tequila, 1 tablespoon honey, 1 tablespoon lime juice, and 1 teaspoon grated lime zest into finished chili with cilantro.

MAKING BLACK BEAN CHILI IN A PRESSURE COOKER

We usually salt-soak beans, but here the extended cooking time of unsoaked beans means we have more time to develop flavor, and more busted beans gave the chili a thick texture. Before adding the beans to the pot, pick through the beans to remove any stones, then give them a quick rinse.

To give this chili a deeper flavor, we rely on the *umami* quality of mushrooms. This savory flavor is produced by an amino acid known as glutamate, which mushrooms happen to have in spades. One pound of mushrooms adds a savory hit to this chili.

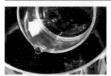
To keep this recipe vegetarian, we rely on equal amounts of vegetable broth and water for the liquid component. Cutting the broth with water prevents the soup from tasting overly sweet and tinny.

We like the addition of red bell peppers to this chili for both their sweet flavor and a little color, but they can't withstand the long cooking time of the beans, so we simmer them in the chili for a few minutes before serving.

TROUBLESHOOTING

Can I double this recipe?	Not if you are using a 6-quart pressure cooker; it won't fit. For an 8-quart pressure cooker, you can increase the recipe by half. Follow the same procedure, but increase the simmering time in step 4 to 25 to 30 minutes.
Do I need to alter the recipe for a 6-quart electric pressure cooker?	Yes, quick release the pressure immediately after the pressurized cooking time; do not let the cooker switch to the warm setting. Increase the simmering time to 20 minutes in step 4, and use the browning (not the simmer) setting.

Garden Vegetable Black Bean Chili
Add 1 zucchini, quartered lengthwise and sliced ½ inch thick, 1 cup frozen corn, and 1 large chopped tomato to pot with bell pepper. Simmer as needed to thicken before serving.

Black Bean and Sausage Chili
Omit mushrooms. Add 1 pound kielbasa sausage, sliced ½ inch thick, and 8 ounces andouille sausage, cut into ½-inch pieces, to pot with broth.

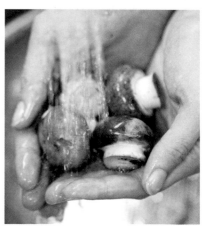

ONE-POT PASTAS AND PASTA SAUCES

Macaroni and Cheese

WHY THIS RECIPE WORKS

For mac and cheese, you're usually stuck with two options: the stuff from the box, which is fast but tastes pasty and artificial; or, the lusciously cheesy casserole style that requires multiple steps of building the sauce, boiling the pasta, then marrying the two and baking it altogether. With our pressure cooker, we discovered we could have from-scratch mac and cheese ready in 20 minutes, and it could all be done in a single pot. We combined macaroni, water, salt, dry mustard, and cayenne and cooked it under pressure for 5 minutes. Since the dairy curdled when cooked under pressure, we waited to add it until after we released the pressure. Evaporated milk thickened the sauce, and a combination of cheddar and Monterey Jack, stirred in a few handfuls at a time, melted perfectly for a flavorful, super-cheesy mac and cheese.

INGREDIENTS

- 8 ounces (2 cups) elbow macaroni
- 2 cups water
  Salt and pepper
- 1 teaspoon dry mustard
  Pinch cayenne pepper
- 1 (12-ounce) can evaporated milk
- 4 ounces sharp cheddar cheese, shredded (1 cup)
- 4 ounces Monterey Jack cheese, shredded (1 cup)

1. HIGH PRESSURE FOR 5 MINUTES: Mix macaroni, water, 1 teaspoon salt, mustard,

SERVES	TOTAL TIME
4	ABOUT 20 MINUTES

PRESSURE LEVEL	RELEASE
HIGH	QUICK

5 MINUTES
UNDER PRESSURE

and cayenne together in pressure-cooker pot. Lock pressure-cooker lid in place and bring to high pressure over medium-high heat. As soon as pot reaches high pressure, reduce heat to medium-low and cook for 5 minutes, adjusting heat as needed to maintain high pressure.

2. QUICK RELEASE PRESSURE: Remove pot from heat. Quick release pressure, then carefully remove lid, allowing steam to escape away from you.

3. BEFORE SERVING: Stir in evaporated milk and simmer over medium-high heat until sauce has thickened and pasta is tender, 1 to 3 minutes. Off heat, stir in cheddar and Monterey Jack cheeses, a handful at a time, until cheese has melted and sauce is smooth. Season with salt and pepper to taste. Serve.

VARIATIONS

Mac and Cheese with Tomatoes
Add 1 (15-ounce) can drained diced tomatoes to pot with macaroni.

Mac and Cheese with Ham and Peas
Stir 8 ounces diced ham steak and ½ cup frozen peas into pot with evaporated milk.

Mac and Cheese with Kielbasa and Mustard
Stir 8 ounces kielbasa sausage, cut into ½-inch pieces, and 4 teaspoons whole-grain Dijon mustard into pot with evaporated milk.

MAKING MAC AND CHEESE IN A PRESSURE COOKER

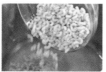
Cooking the pasta under pressure is a huge timesaver since you don't have to wait for a huge pot of water to come to a boil first. Combine the raw macaroni with 2 cups of water and the seasonings in the pressure-cooker pot. All it needs is 5 minutes under pressure.

Cooking dairy under pressure doesn't work because it will curdle. So we stir the dairy into the pot after the pasta has cooked, then simmer the mixture together for a few minutes, uncovered, until it's thickened. Evaporated milk creates a silky, creamy sauce without the work of making a roux.

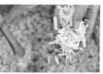
Stirring in the shredded cheese a handful at a time prevents it from clumping. We use a combination of sharp cheddar and Monterey Jack for their combined rich flavor and meltability.

TROUBLESHOOTING

Can I substitute mild or extra-sharp cheddar for the sharp cheddar?	Yes, but we've found that extra-sharp cheddar can take on a grainier texture when melted, so the sauce may not be as creamy. Extra-sharp can sometimes taste a tad saltier, so season carefully. We don't recommend using farmhouse or clothbound cheddar here because neither melt well.
Can I use a different type of pasta?	You can substitute 8 ounces mini shells for the macaroni if desired; larger shapes like rotini and medium or large shells won't work because they don't cook through quickly enough.
Can I use low-fat evaporated milk?	Yes, 2 percent low-fat evaporated milk produces very good results. It might be looser, but you can simmer a little longer or let the dish sit for a few minutes to reach the right consistency. We don't recommend nonfat evaporated milk.
Do I need to alter the recipe for a 6-quart electric pressure cooker?	Yes, instead of relying on the cooker's built-in timer to keep track of the pressurized cooking time, use your own timer and start the countdown as soon as the pot comes to pressure. After the 5-minute cooking time, quick release the pressure immediately; do not let the cooker switch to the warm setting. Use the browning (not the simmer) setting to simmer the sauce in step 3.

Easy Ziti with Sausage and Peppers

WHY THIS RECIPE WORKS

For a one-pot pasta dinner that was streamlined without sacrificing flavor, we started by browning Italian sausage, onion, and green bell pepper just until the sausage was no longer pink. Then we stirred in tomato sauce, water, and our pasta. Using jarred sauce kept things simple, while a tubular pasta like ziti proved to be the best match for the pressure cooker—we learned that strand pasta turns into unappealing clumps of noodles when cooked under pressure. Cooking the ziti for 5 minutes was the best approach to ensure we didn't accidentally overcook the pasta (since we couldn't check for doneness along the way). After 5 minutes, we quick released pressure and let it all simmer for a few minutes to finish cooking the pasta through and concentrate the sauce's flavors. A sprinkling of basil at the end made the right fresh finish for our saucy, meaty ziti dinner. Garnish with Parmesan if desired.

INGREDIENTS

- 1 tablespoon olive oil
- 1 pound hot or sweet Italian sausage, casings removed
- 1 onion, chopped fine
- 1 green bell pepper, stemmed, seeded, and cut into ¾-inch pieces
- 1 (25-ounce) jar tomato sauce
- 3½ cups water
- 1 pound ziti
- 2 tablespoons chopped fresh basil Salt and pepper

SERVES	TOTAL TIME	
4 TO 6	**ABOUT 30 MINUTES**	**5 MINUTES**
PRESSURE LEVEL	RELEASE	
HIGH	**QUICK**	**UNDER PRESSURE**

1. BUILD FLAVOR: Heat oil in pressure-cooker pot over medium-high heat until shimmering. Stir in sausage, onion, and bell pepper and cook, breaking up meat with wooden spoon, until sausage is no longer pink, about 5 minutes. Stir in tomato sauce, water, and ziti.

2. HIGH PRESSURE FOR 5 MINUTES: Lock pressure-cooker lid in place and bring to high pressure over medium-high heat. As soon as pot reaches high pressure, reduce heat to medium-low and cook for 5 minutes, adjusting heat as needed to maintain high pressure.

3. QUICK RELEASE PRESSURE: Remove pot from heat. Quick release pressure, then carefully remove lid, allowing steam to escape away from you.

4. BEFORE SERVING: Bring mixture to simmer over medium-high heat and cook, stirring often, until pasta is tender, 2 to 5 minutes. Stir in basil and season with salt and pepper to taste. Serve.

VARIATION
Ziti with Chicken, Peppers, and Olives
Omit sausage; cook onion and bell pepper until softened, about 5 minutes. Add 2 (6- to 8-ounce) boneless, skinless trimmed chicken breasts to pot with ziti and water in step 1; cook as directed. After releasing pressure, remove chicken, let cool slightly, then shred into bite-size pieces. Stir in shredded chicken and 1 cup pitted and halved kalamata olives to pot with basil.

TEST KITCHEN TIP COOKING SAUSAGE IN A PRESSURE COOKER
Italian sausage is sold in several forms, including links (which is most common), bulk-style tubes, and patties. If you purchase links, you just need to remove the meat from the casing before cooking so that it can crumble into bite-size pieces.

1. Hold sausage firmly on one end and squeeze sausage out of casing through opposite end.

2. Before cooking under pressure, cook sausage with onion and bell pepper, breaking up sausage with wooden spoon into bite-size pieces, until sausage is no longer pink.

TROUBLESHOOTING

Can I use other types of pasta?	Another large tubular pasta, like penne, ziti rigate, and rigatoni, will work fine here. Do not use strand pasta, such as spaghetti or linguine, because the strands clump together into a sticky mess when cooked under pressure.
Can I use chicken sausage?	Yes, you can substitute raw turkey or chicken Italian sausage, removed from its casing. If the sausage is not raw, simply slice it into ¼-inch-thick rounds and increase the amount of oil to 2 tablespoons and continue with the recipe as directed.
Do I need to alter the recipe for a 6-quart electric pressure cooker?	Yes, instead of relying on the cooker's built-in timer to keep track of the pressurized cooking time, use your own timer and start the countdown as soon as the pot comes to pressure. After the 5-minute cooking time, quick release the pressure immediately; do not let the cooker switch to the warm setting. Use the browning (not the simmer) setting to simmer the pasta in step 4.

Weeknight Meat Sauce with Rigatoni

SERVES	TOTAL TIME
4 TO 6	**ABOUT 45 MINUTES**

PRESSURE LEVEL	RELEASE
HIGH	**QUICK**

5 MINUTES
UNDER PRESSURE

✔ WHY THIS RECIPE WORKS

For a quick sauce with the flavors of a Bolognese, we limited the meat to ground beef and chose a pasta shape that we could cook in the pot with the sauce for a one-dish supper. For meatier flavor and texture, we also added mushrooms that we pulsed in the food processor to ensure they blended with the meat. Onion, red pepper flakes, oregano, and garlic gave our sauce the right flavor profile. Crushed tomatoes helped build the base of our sauce, while a smaller can of diced tomatoes added the right texture. We found an additional 3½ cups of water was needed to cook the pasta under pressure. To ensure we didn't overcook the pasta, we kept the cooking time to 5 minutes, which gave us rigatoni that was just al dente. Then we removed the lid and briefly simmered the pasta to a perfect degree of doneness. Garnish with Parmesan if desired.

INGREDIENTS

  2 **ounces cremini mushrooms, trimmed and halved**
  1 **tablespoon olive oil**
  1 **onion, chopped fine**
     Salt and pepper
  3 **garlic cloves, minced**
  ¼ **teaspoon red pepper flakes**
  1 **tablespoon minced fresh oregano or 1 teaspoon dried**
  1 **tablespoon tomato paste**
  1 **pound 85 percent lean ground beef**
3½ **cups water**

1 **(28-ounce) can crushed tomatoes**
1 **(14.5-ounce) can diced tomatoes, drained**
1 **pound rigatoni**
3 **tablespoons chopped fresh basil**

1. PREP MUSHROOMS: Pulse mushrooms in food processor until finely chopped, about 8 pulses, scraping down bowl as needed; transfer to bowl.

2. BUILD FLAVOR: Heat oil in pressure-cooker pot over medium-high heat until shimmering. Add processed mushrooms, onion, and ¼ teaspoon salt and cook until vegetables are softened and well browned, 6 to 12 minutes. Stir in garlic, pepper flakes, oregano, and tomato paste and cook until fragrant, about 1 minute. Stir in ground beef and cook, breaking up meat with wooden spoon, until no longer pink, about 3 minutes. Stir in water, crushed tomatoes, and diced tomatoes, scraping up any browned bits. Stir in pasta.

3. HIGH PRESSURE FOR 5 MINUTES: Lock pressure-cooker lid in place and bring to high pressure over medium-high heat. As soon as pot reaches high pressure, reduce heat to medium-low and cook for 5 minutes, adjusting heat as needed to maintain high pressure.

4. QUICK RELEASE PRESSURE: Remove pot from heat. Quick release pressure, then carefully remove lid, allowing steam to escape away from you.

TEST KITCHEN TIP CLEANING MUSHROOMS
Adding a few ounces of mushrooms is a great way to boost heft and meatiness in both meat-based and vegetarian recipes.

Rinse mushrooms under cold water just before cooking; if done too far in advance, exterior of mushrooms will turn slimy.

TROUBLESHOOTING

Can I use other types of pasta in this recipe?	Another large tubular pasta, such as penne, ziti rigate, or rigatoni, will work fine here. Do not use strand pasta, such as spaghetti or linguine, because the strands clump together into a sticky mess when cooked under pressure.
Can I substitute other types of ground meat?	Yes. You can substitute ground pork or turkey for the beef. We don't recommend using ground chicken or 99 percent lean ground turkey because they are just too lean and will taste dry and mealy in the final dish.
Do I need to alter the recipe for a 6-quart electric pressure cooker?	Yes, instead of relying on the cooker's built-in timer to keep track of the pressurized cooking time, use your own timer and start the countdown as soon as the pot comes to pressure. After the 5-minute cooking time, quick release the pressure immediately; do not let the cooker switch to the warm setting. Use the browning (not the simmer) setting to simmer the pasta in step 5.

5. BEFORE SERVING: Bring to simmer and continue to cook, stirring often, until pasta is nearly al dente, 2 to 5 minutes. Stir in basil and season with salt and pepper to taste. Serve.

Tex-Mex Chili Mac

SERVES	TOTAL TIME
4	**ABOUT 45 MINUTES**

PRESSURE LEVEL	RELEASE
HIGH	**QUICK**

5
MINUTES
UNDER PRESSURE

✔ WHY THIS RECIPE WORKS

For a hearty, meaty macaroni dinner with a kick, we started by sautéing some onion and bell pepper. Stirring in garlic, chili powder, and cayenne and sautéing them briefly helped bloom the spices' flavors and mellow their raw, harsh notes. Next, we added our ground beef and cooked it just until no longer pink. A can of tomato sauce plus some water gave our recipe the right saucy consistency and balancing acidity, and the combination of the two provided the right amount of liquid for cooking the pasta under pressure. The macaroni needed just 5 minutes to cook through. After we removed the lid, green chiles went into the pot, adding the quintessential Tex-Mex zing, and corn added color, sweetness, and good texture. Cilantro and a sprinkling of a shredded Mexican cheese blend made the perfect finish.

INGREDIENTS

- 1 tablespoon vegetable oil
- 1 onion, chopped fine
- 1 green bell pepper, stemmed, seeded, and cut into ½-inch pieces
- 3 garlic cloves, minced
- 2 tablespoons chili powder
- ⅛ teaspoon cayenne pepper
- 1 pound 85 percent lean ground beef
- 2 cups water
- 1 (15-ounce) can tomato sauce
- 8 ounces (2 cups) elbow macaroni
- 1 cup frozen corn

1   **(4.5-ounce) can chopped green chiles**
2   **tablespoons minced fresh cilantro**
    Salt and pepper
4   **ounces shredded Mexican cheese blend (1 cup)**

1. BUILD FLAVOR: Heat oil in pressure-cooker pot over medium-high heat until shimmering. Add onion and bell pepper and cook until softened, 5 to 7 minutes. Stir in garlic, chili powder, and cayenne and cook until fragrant, about 30 seconds. Stir in ground beef and cook, breaking up meat with wooden spoon, until no longer pink, 3 to 5 minutes. Stir in water, tomato sauce, and macaroni.

2. HIGH PRESSURE FOR 5 MINUTES: Lock pressure-cooker lid in place and bring to high pressure over medium-high heat. As soon as pot reaches high pressure, reduce heat to medium-low and cook for 5 minutes, adjusting heat as needed to maintain high pressure.

3. QUICK RELEASE PRESSURE: Remove pot from heat. Quick release pressure, then carefully remove lid, allowing steam to escape away from you.

4. BEFORE SERVING: Stir in corn and chiles and simmer over medium-high heat until corn is heated through and pasta is tender, 1 to 3 minutes. Stir in cilantro and season with salt and pepper to taste. Sprinkle individual portions with shredded cheese before serving.

TEST KITCHEN TIP PREPPING CILANTRO

Unlike parsley, the stems of cilantro are sweet, so you don't have to remove the leaves from the stems before chopping.

After trimming stems and washing cilantro, chop leaves and stems together to get amount called for in recipe.

TROUBLESHOOTING

Can I use fresh corn instead of frozen?	Absolutely. In fact, we think the flavor of fresh corn is superior to that of frozen corn when it is in season and just picked. Substitute raw corn kernels cut from 1 large ear fresh corn for the frozen corn; the cooking time will remain the same.
Can I substitute another cheese for the Mexican cheese blend?	Yes, any mild, good-melting cheese will work fine. Mexican cheese blend is a combination of Colby, sharp cheddar, and Monterey Jack, so any of those would work well alone or in combination. We also like pepper Jack.
Can I use jarred tomato sauce instead of canned?	Canned tomato sauce works best here because it has a smooth texture and is mildly seasoned; most jarred sauce is given an Italian flavor profile (basil, oregano, garlic) that would taste out of place in this Tex-Mex dish. If necessary, you can substitute 1¾ cups of tomato puree, but be ready to season the dish quite liberally before serving.
Do I need to alter the recipe for a 6-quart electric pressure cooker?	Yes, instead of relying on the cooker's built-in timer to keep track of the pressurized cooking time, use your own timer and start the countdown as soon as the pot comes to pressure. After the 5-minute cooking time, quick release the pressure immediately; do not let the cooker switch to the warm setting. Use the browning (not the simmer) setting to simmer the corn and chiles in step 4.

4/13/16 easy delicious made on weeknight
— double meat if can't have

Spook amount of leftover sauce

Meatballs and Marinara

WHY THIS RECIPE WORKS

The key to cooking meatballs in a pressure cooker is making them sturdy so that they don't bust or turn mushy. Starting with meatloaf mix, we tested using various proportions of milk (for moisture) and bread crumbs (for binding power) until we got the texture just right. We found these meatballs needed half the milk and bread crumbs you find in a traditional recipe, and using flaky panko bread crumbs worked best. As for the marinara, we kept the ingredients simple, with onion, crushed tomatoes, oregano, garlic, and red pepper flakes. Cooking the meatballs in the sauce brought all the flavors together.

INGREDIENTS

- 2 tablespoons olive oil
- 1 onion, minced
   Salt and pepper
- 2 tablespoons minced fresh oregano or 2 teaspoons dried
- ¼ teaspoon red pepper flakes
- 6 garlic cloves, minced
- 2 (28-ounce) cans crushed tomatoes
   Sugar
- ½ cup panko bread crumbs
- ¼ cup whole milk
- 1 pound meatloaf mix
- 1 ounce Parmesan cheese, grated (½ cup)
- 3 tablespoons minced fresh parsley
- 1 large egg, lightly beaten
- ¼ cup chopped fresh basil

MAKES	TOTAL TIME	
4 CUPS*	**ABOUT 45 MINUTES**	**5 MINUTES**
PRESSURE LEVEL	RELEASE	**UNDER PRESSURE**
HIGH	**QUICK**	

*ENOUGH FOR 1 POUND OF PASTA

1. BUILD FLAVOR: Heat oil in pressure-cooker pot over medium-high heat until shimmering. Add onion and ¼ teaspoon salt and cook until softened, about 5 minutes. Stir in oregano, red pepper flakes, and two-thirds of garlic and cook until fragrant, about 30 seconds. Stir in crushed tomatoes, scraping up any browned bits. Reduce heat to medium-low and simmer gently, stirring occasionally, until tomatoes no longer taste raw, about 10 minutes. Season with sugar, salt, and pepper to taste.

2. Meanwhile, mash panko and milk into paste in medium bowl with fork. Gently mix in meatloaf mix, Parmesan, parsley, egg, remaining garlic, ¾ teaspoon salt, and ½ teaspoon pepper with hands until thoroughly combined. Shape mixture into 12 even-size meatballs. Gently nestle meatballs into sauce.

3. HIGH PRESSURE FOR 5 MINUTES: Lock pressure-cooker lid in place and bring to high pressure over medium-high heat. As soon as pot reaches high pressure, reduce heat to medium-low and cook for 5 minutes, adjusting heat as needed to maintain high pressure.

4. QUICK RELEASE PRESSURE: Remove pot from heat. Quick release pressure, then carefully remove lid, allowing steam to escape away from you.

5. BEFORE SERVING: Stir in basil and season with additional sugar, salt, and pepper to taste. Serve.

MAKING MEATBALLS IN A PRESSURE COOKER

In most recipes, we simmer the sauce mixture to drive off the tinny flavor from the canned tomatoes and to deepen their flavor at the end of cooking. But here, we do it first to minimize jostling the tender meatballs once they are in the pot. Once it's cooked down, we season our sauce.

We use our hands to mix the meatball mixture together since using a spatula or spoon doesn't mix the milk-panko mixture and the egg into the meat evenly. We also use our hands to divide and shape the mixture into meatballs. It's important to pack them well so that they don't bust apart under pressure.

Gently nestle the raw meatballs into the sauce so that they can soak up some of the flavor of the sauce and likewise infuse the sauce with some meaty flavor. For even cooking, arrange them in the pot in a single layer. After 5 minutes and a quick release, they're cooked through.

TROUBLESHOOTING

What if I can't find meatloaf mix?	You can substitute ½ pound each 85 percent lean ground beef and ground pork.
Can I use bread crumbs that aren't panko?	Yes, you can substitute ⅓ cup dried, unseasoned bread crumbs, but the resulting meatballs will have a slightly breadier texture.
Can I make the meatballs ahead of time?	Yes, you can shape them and refrigerate them on a parchment-lined baking sheet, covered loosely with plastic wrap, for up to 6 hours, then cook as directed.
Do I need to alter the recipe for a 6-quart electric pressure cooker?	Yes, use the browning (not the simmer) setting to simmer the sauce in step 1. Instead of relying on the cooker's built-in timer to keep track of the pressurized cooking time, use your own timer and start the countdown as soon as the pot comes to pressure. After the 5-minute cooking time, quick release the pressure immediately; do not let the cooker switch to the warm setting.

Bolognese

Bolognese is typically a labor of love, involving a long shopping list, a lot of prep, and hours spent at the stove. For this version, we started with meatloaf mix, which was an easy way to add lots of meaty flavor from beef, pork, and veal, sold in one simple package. A few ounces each of mortadella and pancetta gave our sauce a richness to take it to the next level. To quickly break down our classic Italian aromatic *soffritto* base of onion, celery, and carrot, as well as the mortadella and pancetta, we turned to our food processor. We added the meatloaf mix to the pot first, to cook off moisture. Once it began to sizzle, we knew it was time to sauté the soffritto and other meats in the rendered fat, building another layer of deep flavor. Then our pressure cooker came into play. We added our wine and broth to the pot, locked on the lid, and cooked our sauce for just 30 minutes. The end result was a sauce with concentrated, rich flavor that tasted like it had been cooked all day. Garnish with Parmesan if desired.

INGREDIENTS

- 1   **onion, chopped coarse**
- 1   **large carrot, peeled and chopped coarse**
- 1   **celery rib, chopped coarse**
- 4   **ounces pancetta, chopped**
- 4   **ounces mortadella, chopped**
- 3   **tablespoons olive oil**
- 1   **pound meatloaf mix**

MAKES	TOTAL TIME	
4 CUPS*	**ABOUT 1½ HOURS**	**30**
PRESSURE LEVEL	RELEASE	**MINUTES**
HIGH	**QUICK**	**UNDER PRESSURE**

*ENOUGH FOR 1 POUND OF PASTA

3 tablespoons minced fresh sage
1 (6-ounce) can tomato paste
1 cup dry red wine
2 cups beef broth
Salt and pepper

1. PREP INGREDIENTS: Pulse onion, carrot, and celery in food processor until finely chopped, about 10 pulses; transfer to bowl. Pulse pancetta and mortadella in now-empty food processor until finely chopped, about 25 pulses; transfer to separate bowl.

2. BUILD FLAVOR: Heat oil in pressure-cooker pot over medium-high heat until shimmering. Add meatloaf mix and cook, breaking up pieces with spoon, until all liquid has evaporated and meat begins to sizzle, 10 to 15 minutes. Stir in processed pancetta mixture and sage, reduce heat to medium, and cook, stirring often, until pancetta is translucent, 5 to 7 minutes. Stir in processed vegetables and tomato paste and cook, stirring often, until mixture is rust-colored and fragrant, about 3 minutes. Stir in wine, scraping up any browned bits, and cook until slightly thickened, about 3 minutes. Stir in beef broth.

3. HIGH PRESSURE FOR 30 MINUTES: Lock pressure-cooker lid in place and bring to high pressure over medium-high heat. As soon as pot reaches high pressure, reduce heat to medium-low and cook for 30 minutes, adjusting heat as needed to maintain high pressure.

MAKING BOLOGNESE IN A PRESSURE COOKER

The trio of onion, celery, and carrot makes up a classic soffritto, which is used in this Italian recipe (and many others) to add flavor. We finely chop the vegetables in the food processor to ensure they melt into the sauce.

We also chop pancetta and mortadella in the food processor. These two components lend a lot of concentrated, meaty flavor to the final sauce.

We wait to add the soffritto and chopped meats to the pot until after we've sauteed the meatloaf mix. Cooking off the liquid released by the meatloaf mix before adding the vegetables ensures the vegetables' flavor isn't watered down and the texture doesn't become bloated.

The last steps are to quick release the pressure and simmer the sauce for 10 minutes more so that it cooks down to the right consistency.

TROUBLESHOOTING

What if I can't find meatloaf mix? You can substitute ½ pound each 85 percent lean ground beef and ground pork.

What kind of wine works best here? Use a good-quality medium-bodied wine, such as a Côtes du Rhône or Pinot Noir.

Do I need to alter the recipe for a 6-quart electric pressure cooker? Yes, quick release the pressure immediately after the pressurized cooking time; do not let the cooker switch to the warm setting. Increase the simmering time to 20 minutes in step 5, and use the browning (not the simmer) setting.

4. QUICK RELEASE PRESSURE: Remove pot from heat. Quick release pressure, then carefully remove lid, allowing steam to escape away from you.

5. BEFORE SERVING: Bring sauce to simmer over medium-high heat and cook until thickened, about 10 minutes. Season with salt and pepper to taste. Serve.

Pork Ragu

WHY THIS RECIPE WORKS

With its ability to tenderize meat and concentrate flavors in minimal time, the pressure cooker achieves the complex, rich flavor and ultratender meat of a traditional slow-simmered Italian ragu in just 20 minutes. Once cooked, our boneless country-style pork ribs needed just a nudge with the end of a spoon to break into shreds. Cooking some aromatics, red wine, and tomato paste in the pot before adding the meat gave our sauce depth and an acidic element, while a can of crushed tomatoes gave it the right chunky ragu-like consistency. Because the meat releases a fair amount of liquid, we simmered the sauce for five minutes to deepen the flavor and thicken the sauce. Serve with a short, tubular pasta such as penne, rigatoni, or ziti.

INGREDIENTS

1½   **pounds boneless country-style pork ribs, trimmed and cut into 1-inch pieces**
    Salt and pepper
1   **tablespoon vegetable oil**
1   **onion, chopped fine**
6   **garlic cloves, minced**
1½   **tablespoons tomato paste**
1   **teaspoon dried oregano**
⅛   **teaspoon red pepper flakes**
½   **cup dry red wine**
1   **(28-ounce) can crushed tomatoes**
¾   **cup low-sodium chicken broth**
2   **tablespoons minced fresh parsley**

MAKES	TOTAL TIME
5 CUPS*	**ABOUT 1¼ HOURS**
PRESSURE LEVEL	RELEASE
HIGH	**NATURAL**

*ENOUGH FOR 1 POUND OF PASTA

20 MINUTES
UNDER PRESSURE

1. BUILD FLAVOR: Pat pork dry with paper towels and season with salt and pepper. Heat oil in pressure-cooker pot over medium-high heat until just smoking. Add half of pork and brown lightly on all sides, about 5 minutes. Stir in onion and cook until onion is softened and pork is well browned, about 5 minutes. Stir in garlic, tomato paste, oregano, and pepper flakes and cook until fragrant, about 30 seconds. Stir in wine, scraping up any browned bits, and simmer until nearly evaporated, about 2 minutes. Stir in tomatoes, broth, and remaining pork.

2. HIGH PRESSURE FOR 20 MINUTES: Lock pressure-cooker lid in place and bring to high pressure over medium-high heat. As soon as pot reaches high pressure, reduce heat to medium-low and cook for 20 minutes, adjusting heat as needed to maintain high pressure.

3. NATURALLY RELEASE PRESSURE: Remove pot from heat and allow pressure to release naturally for 15 minutes. Quick release any remaining pressure, then carefully remove lid, allowing steam to escape away from you.

4. BEFORE SERVING: Using large spoon, skim excess fat from surface of sauce. Break meat into bite-size pieces with spoon. Bring sauce to simmer over medium-high heat and cook until slightly thickened, about 5 minutes. Stir in parsley and season with salt and pepper to taste. Serve.

MAKING PORK RAGU IN A PRESSURE COOKER

Country-style pork ribs are perfect for our ragu because they cook quickly and have good flavor and a moist texture. You can buy them in conveniently small quantities, and because they are boneless they are easy to cut into uniform pieces. Trim off any excess fat, then cut the ribs into 1-inch pieces.

It's important to sauté the aromatics—garlic, tomato paste, and red pepper flakes—before adding the liquid. We sauté them after browning the meat and onions so that they pick up more flavor. Just 30 seconds of cooking them gets the job done.

After stirring in the wine and scraping up the fond, add your cooking liquid: broth and tomatoes. Brand matters here, as different brands have dramatically different textures and can have a big effect on the final texture of the sauce; we use Tuttorosso Crushed Tomatoes in Thick Puree with Basil.

Country-style ribs render a fair amount of fat into the sauce, so after cooking, we skim fat from the surface before breaking the meat up into bite-size pieces and reducing the sauce to the proper consistency.

TROUBLESHOOTING

Can I use a different cut of pork?

Yes, you can substitute 1½ pounds of boneless pork shoulder, trimmed and cut into 1-inch pieces; increase the pressurized cooking time to 25 minutes. Do not use lean cuts like boneless pork chops, pork tenderloin, or pork loin roast, however, because they will overcook.

Can I double this recipe?

Yes, it can be doubled whether you are using a 6-quart or an 8-quart pot. In both cases, you will need to increase the pressurized cooking time to 30 minutes. You might also want to simmer the sauce a little longer in step 4.

Do I need to alter the recipe for a 6-quart electric pressure cooker?

Yes, turn the cooker off immediately after the pressurized cooking time and let the pressure release naturally for 15 minutes; do not let the cooker switch to the warm setting. Increase the simmering time to 15 minutes in step 4, and use the browning (not the simmer) setting.

Beef Ragu with Warm Spices

MAKES	TOTAL TIME
4 CUPS*	**ABOUT 1½ HOURS**

PRESSURE LEVEL	RELEASE
HIGH	**NATURAL**

25 MINUTES
UNDER PRESSURE

*ENOUGH FOR 1 POUND OF PASTA

✔ WHY THIS RECIPE WORKS

For a new spin on classic ragu, we started by swapping in well-marbled beef short ribs for the pork. Leaving the meat on the bones for cooking meant minimal prep, and the bones helped to naturally thicken the sauce and added meaty depth. We browned them well before bringing the pot up to pressure to maximize the meaty flavor. Once the meat was done, the bones could be pulled out with tongs. For a flavor profile that fit this wintry, comfort-food sauce, we added cinnamon and cloves. To prevent a greasy sauce, make sure to trim as much fat as possible from the ribs before browning them. Serve over egg noodles.

INGREDIENTS

- 1½   **pounds bone-in English-style beef short ribs, trimmed**
-     **Salt and pepper**
- 1   **tablespoon vegetable oil**
- 1   **onion, chopped fine**
- ¼   **teaspoon ground cinnamon**
-     **Pinch ground cloves**
- ½   **cup red wine**
- 1   **(28-ounce) can crushed tomatoes**
- 2   **tablespoons minced fresh parsley**

1. BUILD FLAVOR: Pat ribs dry with paper towels and season with salt and pepper. Heat oil in pressure-cooker pot over medium-high heat until just smoking. Brown ribs well on all sides, 8 to 10 minutes; transfer to plate.

2. Pour off all but 1 teaspoon fat left in pot, add onion, and cook over medium heat until softened, about 5 minutes. Stir in cinnamon and cloves and cook until fragrant, about 30 seconds. Stir in wine, scraping up any browned bits, and simmer until nearly evaporated, about 2 minutes. Stir in tomatoes. Nestle browned ribs with any accumulated juices into sauce.

3. HIGH PRESSURE FOR 25 MINUTES: Lock pressure-cooker lid in place and bring to high pressure over medium-high heat. As soon as pot reaches high pressure, reduce heat to medium-low and cook for 25 minutes, adjusting heat as needed to maintain high pressure.

4. NATURALLY RELEASE PRESSURE: Remove pot from heat and allow pressure to release naturally for 15 minutes. Quick release any remaining pressure, then carefully remove lid, allowing steam to escape away from you.

5. BEFORE SERVING: Transfer ribs to plate, let cool slightly, then shred meat into bite-size pieces, discarding fat and bones. Using large spoon, skim excess fat from surface of sauce. Return shredded meat to sauce, bring to simmer over medium-high heat, and cook until slightly thickened, about 5 minutes. Stir in parsley and season with salt and pepper to taste. Serve.

TEST KITCHEN TIP PREPARING BONE-IN BEEF SHORT RIBS
Short ribs can be very fatty, so it's important to trim them well before cooking to avoid a greasy sauce.

Trim excess hard fat and silverskin from both sides of each short rib using chef's knife.

TROUBLESHOOTING

What if my sauce seems greasy?	Short ribs can be really fatty, so be sure to trim away as much visible fat as possible before browning the ribs. If your sauce still seems greasy after skimming fat from the surface of the sauce in step 5, either you can let the sauce sit a little longer so that more fat rises to the surface for skimming, or you can refrigerate the sauce for a couple of hours. Once refrigerated, more fat will have collected on top of the sauce and turned solid, making it very easy to remove before reheating.
What if my sauce is too watery?	Simply continue to simmer it in step 5 until it has thickened to your desired consistency.
What if my sauce is too thick?	You can stir in beef broth or low-sodium chicken broth to loosen it up to your desired consistency.
Can I double this recipe?	Yes, if you have an 8-quart pressure cooker. If you have a 6-quart pressure cooker, you can't double it, but you can increase the recipe by half. In both cases, brown only one batch of meat, and there's no need to double the oil; the pressurized cooking time will remain the same.
Do I need to alter the recipe for a 6-quart electric pressure cooker?	Yes, add 1 cup of low-sodium chicken broth to the pot with the tomatoes in step 2. Turn the cooker off immediately after the pressurized cooking time and let the pressure release naturally for 15 minutes; do not let the cooker switch to the warm setting. Increase the simmering time to 15 minutes in step 5, and use the browning (not the simmer) setting.

Garden Tomato Sauce

MAKES	TOTAL TIME
3 CUPS*	**ABOUT 1 HOUR**

PRESSURE LEVEL	RELEASE
HIGH	**QUICK**

30 MINUTES
UNDER PRESSURE

*ENOUGH FOR 1 POUND OF PASTA

WHY THIS RECIPE WORKS

For a pasta sauce that makes the most of the bright, fresh flavor and meaty texture of in-season tomatoes but minimizes the work, we started by cooking whole fresh tomatoes in the pressure cooker. We didn't have to blanch and peel the tomatoes like you would in traditional recipes because we discovered after thirty minutes under pressure, we could slip the peels off the softened tomatoes with a pair of tongs. Putting the tomatoes into the pressure cooker cored side down made this a one-step process, while cooking them in red wine and water, plus garlic, tomato paste, and pepper flakes, kept our recipe simple. We used a potato masher to mash the cooked tomatoes to the right saucy but still slightly chunky consistency. To ensure the tomatoes were the star, we kept the seasoning simple. Chopped basil, stirred in just before serving, contributed additional freshness and color. Note that the success of this dish depends on using ultraripe, in-season tomatoes.

INGREDIENTS

- 3 tablespoons olive oil
- 3 garlic cloves, minced
- 1 tablespoon tomato paste
  Pinch red pepper flakes
- ½ cup dry red wine
- ½ cup water
  Salt and pepper
- 3 pounds very ripe, in-season tomatoes, cored
- 2 tablespoons chopped fresh basil

1. BUILD FLAVOR: Cook oil, garlic, tomato paste, and pepper flakes in pressure-cooker pot over medium heat until fragrant, about 1 minute. Stir in wine, water, and 1 teaspoon salt. Arrange tomatoes in pot, cored side down.

2. HIGH PRESSURE FOR 30 MINUTES: Lock pressure-cooker lid in place and bring to high pressure over medium-high heat. As soon as pot reaches high pressure, reduce heat to medium-low and cook for 30 minutes, adjusting heat as needed to maintain high pressure.

3. QUICK RELEASE PRESSURE: Remove pot from heat. Quick release pressure, then carefully remove lid, allowing steam to escape away from you.

4. BEFORE SERVING: Using tongs, remove and discard tomato skins. Mash tomatoes with potato masher until mostly smooth. Bring sauce to simmer over medium-high heat and cook until thickened, 15 to 20 minutes. Stir in basil and season with salt and pepper to taste. Serve.

VARIATIONS

Puttanesca

Increase red pepper flakes to 1 teaspoon. Add 8 rinsed and minced anchovy fillets to pot with oil in step 1. After simmering sauce in step 4, stir in ½ cup pitted and chopped kalamata olives and 3 tablespoons rinsed capers. Substitute ¼ cup minced fresh parsley for basil.

MAKING GARDEN TOMATO SAUCE IN A PRESSURE COOKER

This sauce starts with 3 pounds of tomatoes. The only prep they require is coring. Use a paring knife to remove each core, then arrange the tomatoes in the pot, cored side down. How they're arranged in the pot isn't as much a factor for the cooking time as it is for the next step, removing the skins.

In a traditional recipe, you'd have to peel the tomatoes before cooking. We found that if we cooked the tomatoes whole under pressure, the skins came off the softened tomatoes in one simple move. Once the tomatoes are cooked, use tongs to remove the skins; they should slip off easily.

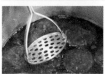
After removing the skins, we mash the tomatoes with a potato masher until they're mostly smooth (you won't be able to get a completely smooth texture), then simmer the sauce for 15–20 minutes to get it to just the right consistency and to deepen the flavor.

TROUBLESHOOTING

Can I double this recipe?	Doubling would overfill the pot. But if you have an 8-quart pressure cooker, you can increase all of the ingredients by half; leave the amount of wine and water the same at ½ cup each. The pressurized cooking time will remain the same.
Can I use plum tomatoes?	Yes, if they are very ripe, plum tomatoes will work fine.
Do I need to alter the recipe for a 6-quart electric pressure cooker?	Yes, quick release the pressure immediately after the pressurized cooking time; do not let the cooker switch to the warm setting. Increase the simmering time to 35 minutes in step 4, and use the browning (not the simmer) setting. Be sure to use a potato masher that won't scratch nonstick surfaces.

Tomato, Vodka, and Cream Sauce

Increase red pepper flakes to ¼ teaspoon. Stir in ¼ cup vodka after simmering sauce for 10 minutes in step 4. Before stirring in basil, stir in ⅓ cup heavy cream and simmer until sauce is thickened, about 2 minutes.

Arrabbiata

Increase red pepper flakes to ½–¾ teaspoon and substitute ¼ cup minced fresh parsley for basil.

Creamy Mushroom Sauce

WHY THIS RECIPE WORKS
When making a creamy mushroom-based pasta sauce, you typically start by sautéing mushrooms to draw out their liquid and concentrate their flavor. In the pressure cooker this happens without any work. After sautéing onion, garlic, and thyme, along with a little flour to thicken the sauce, we whisked in broth and sherry, a classic mushroom complement. We turned to a trio of flavorful mushrooms for our starring ingredient. Less than 30 minutes under pressure was all it took to draw out their liquid and to concentrate their flavor. The mushrooms' liquid, which couldn't evaporate from the pot, became a flavorful component in our sauce. To avoid curdled cream, we stirred it in toward the end. Parmesan cheese helped thicken our sauce and, along with parsley, added a final layer of flavor.

INGREDIENTS

- ¼   cup olive oil
- 1   onion, minced
     Salt and pepper
- 1   tablespoon all-purpose flour
- 3   garlic cloves, minced
- 1   tablespoon minced fresh thyme
     or 1½ teaspoons dried
- 1¼   cups low-sodium chicken
     broth
- ¼   cup dry sherry
- 10   ounces shiitake mushrooms,
     stemmed and sliced thin
- 10   ounces cremini mushrooms,
     trimmed and sliced thin

MAKES	TOTAL TIME
4 CUPS*	**ABOUT 1 HOUR**

PRESSURE LEVEL	RELEASE
HIGH	**QUICK**

*ENOUGH FOR 1 POUND OF PASTA

25 MINUTES
UNDER PRESSURE

10 ounces portobello mushroom caps, gills removed, caps halved and sliced thin

½ cup heavy cream

1 ounce Parmesan cheese, grated (½ cup)

2 tablespoons minced fresh parsley

1. BUILD FLAVOR: Heat oil in pressure-cooker pot over medium heat until shimmering. Add onion and ½ teaspoon salt and cook until softened, about 5 minutes. Stir in flour, garlic, and thyme and cook until fragrant, about 30 seconds. Whisk in broth and sherry, scraping up any browned bits. Stir in mushrooms.

2. HIGH PRESSURE FOR 25 MINUTES: Lock pressure-cooker lid in place and bring to high pressure over medium-high heat. As soon as pot reaches high pressure, reduce heat to medium-low and cook for 25 minutes, adjusting heat as needed to maintain high pressure.

3. QUICK RELEASE PRESSURE: Remove pot from heat. Quick release pressure, then carefully remove lid, allowing steam to escape away from you.

4. BEFORE SERVING: Stir in cream and simmer sauce over medium-high heat until thickened, about 5 minutes. Off heat, stir in Parmesan and parsley. Season with salt and pepper to taste. Serve.

MAKING CREAMY MUSHROOM SAUCE IN A PRESSURE COOKER

After sautéing an onion until softened, we stir in some aromatics, plus flour to help thicken the sauce. Then we whisk in broth and sherry. There will be some browned bits, or fond, on the pot's bottom, so once you've added the liquid, scrape them up and incorporate them into the sauce.

A mix of cremini, shiitake, and portobello mushrooms lend both texture and flavor. Since the gills on the underside of a portobello cap can make a sauce muddy and dark, scrape them off using a soupspoon.

Cream curdles if cooked under pressure, so we wait until after the mushrooms are cooked through under pressure to add it to the pot, then we simmer the sauce for 5 minutes to help it thicken.

Stirring in some Parmesan at the end not only adds a nice salty, cheesy element but also helps to thicken up the sauce just a bit further.

TROUBLESHOOTING

Do I need to use all three types of mushrooms?
We recommend using them all for the deepest flavor and variety of texture, but you could substitute white button mushrooms for either the shiitakes and/or the cremini and increase the simmering time in step 4 to 10 minutes (white button mushrooms tend to release more water). Do not make any substitutions for the portobellos; their meaty flavor and texture are crucial here.

Can I make this recipe vegetarian?
Yes, substitute an equal amount of vegetable broth for the chicken broth.

Do I need to alter the recipe for a 6-quart electric pressure cooker?
Yes, quick release the pressure immediately after the pressurized cooking time; do not let the cooker switch to the warm setting. Increase the simmering time to 15 minutes in step 4, and use the browning (not the simmer) setting.

Braised Chicken in Marinara Sauce

WHY THIS RECIPE WORKS

For our pressure-cooker take on the Italian-American classic chicken and marinara, we started with bone-in chicken breasts since they would stay more moist than boneless breasts during their cooking time. Even though we knew the skin wouldn't brown in the steamy pressure-cooker environment, we left it in place since it would guard the meat from drying out. Cooking the chicken in the sauce infused the meat with the sauce's flavor, and the meat's juices also gave the marinara a boost. Since we wanted to develop a recipe that would require minimal prep, we took store-bought pasta sauce and bolstered it with fresh garlic, tomato paste, and red pepper flakes prior to cooking, and just before serving we stirred in some Parmesan and fresh basil. Serve over pasta (or rice) or with a fresh loaf of Italian or French bread. Our favorite brand of jarred marinara is Victoria Marinara Sauce.

INGREDIENTS

- 1   tablespoon olive oil
- 5   garlic cloves, minced
- 2   tablespoons tomato paste
- ¼   teaspoon red pepper flakes
- 1   cup jarred marinara sauce
- 4   (12-ounce) bone-in split chicken breasts, trimmed
     Salt and pepper
- 1   ounce Parmesan cheese, grated (½ cup)
- 2   tablespoons chopped fresh basil

SERVES	TOTAL TIME
4	ABOUT 40 MINUTES

PRESSURE LEVEL	RELEASE
HIGH	QUICK

15 MINUTES
UNDER PRESSURE

1. BUILD FLAVOR: Cook oil, garlic, tomato paste, and pepper flakes in pressure-cooker pot over medium-high heat until fragrant, about 1 minute. Stir in marinara sauce, scraping up any browned bits. Season chicken with salt and pepper and nestle into pot.

2. HIGH PRESSURE FOR 15 MINUTES: Lock pressure-cooker lid in place and bring to high pressure over medium-high heat. As soon as pot reaches high pressure, reduce heat to medium-low and cook for 15 minutes, adjusting heat as needed to maintain high pressure.

3. QUICK RELEASE PRESSURE: Remove pot from heat. Quick release pressure, then carefully remove lid, allowing steam to escape away from you.

4. BEFORE SERVING: Transfer chicken to serving dish and remove skin. Tent chicken loosely with aluminum foil and let rest for 5 minutes. Using large spoon, skim excess fat from surface of sauce. Stir in Parmesan and basil and season with salt and pepper to taste. Pour sauce over chicken and serve.

TEST KITCHEN TIP TRIMMING BONE-IN CHICKEN BREASTS

To ensure even cooking and to prevent the need for skimming rendered fat from the finished dish, we've found in general it's best to trim rib section bones from chicken breasts before cooking. This also allows multiple chicken breasts to easily fit in the pot.

Using kitchen shears, trim off rib section from each breast, following vertical line of fat from tapered end of breast up to socket where the wing was attached.

TROUBLESHOOTING

How can I be sure the chicken is cooked through?	We feel confident the chicken will be cooked through, but you can check for doneness using a thermometer; the thickest part of the breast should register 160 degrees. If it's underdone, gently simmer it in the sauce until it registers 160 degrees. Add water to the pot if the sauce cooks down too much.
Does it matter if my chicken breasts are not 12 ounces?	Surprisingly, no. We tested this recipe using chicken breasts than measured between 10½ and 15 ounces each (before trimming), and they all were properly cooked in 15 minutes. However, if your chicken breasts are very small, weighing less than 10 ounces, you might want to reduce the pressurized cooking time by a couple of minutes.
Can I substitute boneless, skinless chicken?	Yes, but they might cook up a bit drier than bone-in breasts; you will need to reduce the pressurized cooking time to 8 minutes.
Do I need to alter the recipe for a 6-quart electric pressure cooker?	Yes, quick release the pressure immediately after the pressurized cooking time; do not let the cooker switch to the warm setting.

Rustic Braised Chicken with Mushrooms

WHY THIS RECIPE WORKS

Using chunks of mushrooms, tomatoes, and bacon was a great start for a rustic sauce for bone-in chicken breasts, but it took some work to build a sauce that would cling to the chicken and lightly coat a bed of noodles or rice. By the end of cooking under pressure, the mushrooms had released enough liquid to make the sauce too loose. Adding a slurry of cornstarch and water after releasing the pressure gave our sauce the right amount of cling. Stirring in some fresh parsley at the end added a fresh note and rounded out this rustic meal.

INGREDIENTS

- **6** slices bacon, cut into ½-inch pieces
- **1** onion, chopped fine
- **2** tablespoons tomato paste
- **4** garlic cloves, minced
- **2** teaspoons minced fresh thyme or ½ teaspoon dried
- **⅛** teaspoon red pepper flakes
- **½** cup dry white wine
- **½** cup low-sodium chicken broth
- **1¼** pounds cremini mushrooms, trimmed and halved if small or quartered if large
- **1** (14.5-ounce) can diced tomatoes
- **¼** ounce dried porcini mushrooms, rinsed and minced
- **4** (12-ounce) bone-in split chicken breasts, trimmed (see page 75)

SERVES	TOTAL TIME
4	ABOUT 1 HOUR
PRESSURE LEVEL	RELEASE
HIGH	QUICK

15 MINUTES
UNDER PRESSURE

Salt and pepper

1½ tablespoons cornstarch

1½ tablespoons water

¼ cup minced fresh parsley

1. BUILD FLAVOR: Cook bacon in pressure-cooker pot over medium-high heat until crisp, about 5 minutes. Using slotted spoon, transfer bacon to paper towel–lined plate; pour off all but 1 tablespoon fat from pot.

2. Add onion to fat left in pot and cook over medium heat until softened, about 5 minutes. Stir in tomato paste, garlic, thyme, and pepper flakes and cook until fragrant, about 1 minute. Stir in wine and cook until slightly reduced, about 1 minute. Stir in broth, cremini mushrooms, tomatoes, and porcini mushrooms. Using wooden spoon, scrape up all browned bits stuck on bottom of pot. Season chicken with salt and pepper and lay on top of vegetables.

3. HIGH PRESSURE FOR 15 MINUTES: Lock pressure-cooker lid in place and bring to high pressure over medium-high heat. As soon as pot reaches high pressure, reduce heat to medium-low and cook for 15 minutes, adjusting heat as needed to maintain high pressure.

4. QUICK RELEASE PRESSURE: Remove pot from heat. Quick release pressure, then carefully remove lid, allowing steam to escape away from you.

TEST KITCHEN TIP PREPPING PORCINI FOR THE PRESSURE COOKER

Dried porcini mushrooms are an easy way to add deep mushroom flavor to a dish. Typically we rehydrate them in hot water prior to cooking, but there's no need for this with the pressure cooker, which does a great job of softening their texture and concentrating their flavor even without the soaking step.

Place dried porcini mushrooms in fine-mesh strainer and run under water to remove any grit, using fingers as needed to rub grit out of crevices. Then chop and add to pressure cooker pot.

TROUBLESHOOTING

Can I substitute another mushroom for the cremini?	Yes, you can substitute white mushrooms, or portobello mushrooms, gills removed and cut into 1-inch pieces.
Can I use boneless, skinless chicken breasts in this recipe?	Yes, but you will need to reduce the pressurized cooking time to 8 minutes.
If I don't have bacon, is there a substitute?	Yes, you can substitute 1 tablespoon olive oil to sauté the aromatics in step 2. But note, without the bacon the recipe will lack the smoky undertone.
Do I need to alter the recipe for a 6-quart electric pressure cooker?	Yes, quick release the pressure immediately after the pressurized cooking time; do not let the cooker switch to the warm setting. Use the browning (not the simmer) setting to simmer the sauce in step 5.

5. BEFORE SERVING: Transfer chicken to serving dish and remove skin. Tent chicken loosely with aluminum foil and let rest while finishing sauce. Using large spoon, skim excess fat from surface of sauce, then bring to simmer over medium-high heat. Whisk cornstarch and water together, then whisk into sauce and cook until thickened, about 1 minute. Stir in parsley and season with salt and pepper to taste. Pour sauce over chicken, sprinkle with bacon, and serve.

Braised Chicken Thighs with Potatoes

SERVES	TOTAL TIME
4	ABOUT 1 HOUR

PRESSURE LEVEL	RELEASE
HIGH	QUICK

20 MINUTES
UNDER PRESSURE

✅ WHY THIS RECIPE WORKS

For a chicken and potatoes dinner with a delicately flavored sauce, we started by browning half of the chicken thighs to create some fond in the pressure cooker. We then discarded the skin since we knew it would lose any crispness in the pressure cooker and also lead to a greasy sauce. Next we added onion, then garlic, wine, and broth (plus flour for thickening power), picking up the flavorful browned bits on the bottom of the pot in the process. Nestling the chicken thighs into the sauce and topping them with our potatoes ensured even cooking. After 20 minutes under pressure, our chicken, potatoes, and sauce were done. While the chicken rested, we stirred tarragon into the sauce to give it complexity. We prefer to use red potatoes measuring 1 to 2 inches in diameter here; do not substitute larger potatoes or they will affect the cooking time.

INGREDIENTS

- 8 (5- to 7-ounce) bone-in chicken thighs, trimmed
  Salt and pepper
- 1 tablespoon vegetable oil
- 1 onion, chopped fine
- 3 garlic cloves, minced
- 2 tablespoons all-purpose flour
- ½ cup dry white wine
- ¾ cup low-sodium chicken broth
- 2 pounds small red potatoes, halved
- 1 tablespoon minced fresh tarragon

1. BUILD FLAVOR: Pat chicken dry with paper towels and season with salt and pepper. Heat oil in pressure-cooker pot over medium-high heat until just smoking. Brown half of thighs, skin side down, until golden, about 6 minutes; transfer to plate. Remove and discard skin from browned and unbrowned thighs. Pour off all but 1 tablespoon fat from pot.

2. Add onion to fat left in pot and cook over medium heat until softened, about 5 minutes. Stir in garlic and cook until fragrant, about 30 seconds. Stir in flour and cook for 1 minute. Whisk in wine, smoothing out any lumps, and cook until slightly reduced, about 1 minute. Stir in broth. Using wooden spoon, scrape up all browned bits stuck on bottom of pot. Nestle chicken with any accumulated juices into pot and top with potatoes.

3. HIGH PRESSURE FOR 20 MINUTES: Lock pressure-cooker lid in place and bring to high pressure over medium-high heat. As soon as pot reaches high pressure, reduce heat to medium-low and cook for 20 minutes, adjusting heat as needed to maintain high pressure.

4. QUICK RELEASE PRESSURE: Remove pot from heat. Quick release pressure, then carefully remove lid, allowing steam to escape away from you.

TEST KITCHEN TIP TRIMMING AND REMOVING SKIN FROM CHICKEN THIGHS
To avoid a greasy sauce, we remove the skin from all of the chicken thighs (both browned and unbrowned) before cooking them under pressure.

Using paper towel to help grip skin firmly, remove skin from browned chicken thighs.

TROUBLESHOOTING

Can I substitute bone-in chicken breasts for the thighs?	Yes, you can substitute 4 (12-ounce) bone-in chicken breasts for the thighs; brown all the breasts since they fit in the pot in one batch, and reduce the pressurized cooking time to 15 minutes. Because breasts give off more liquid than thighs, simmer the sauce while the chicken rests to reach the proper consistency.
If my potatoes are bigger than 2 inches, is that OK?	Yes, just cut them into roughly 1-inch pieces before cooking; you may end up with some pieces that break down into the sauce.
Do I need to alter the recipe for a 6-quart electric pressure cooker?	Yes, increase the amount of chicken broth to 1¾ cups. Quick release the pressure immediately after the pressurized cooking time; do not let the cooker switch to the warm setting. Before adding the tarragon in step 5, simmer the sauce for 10 minutes to thicken using the browning (not the simmer) setting.

5. BEFORE SERVING: Transfer potatoes and chicken to serving dish, tent loosely with aluminum foil, and let rest for 5 minutes. Using large spoon, skim excess fat from surface of sauce. Stir in tarragon and season with salt and pepper to taste. Pour sauce over chicken and potatoes and serve.

Easy Chicken and Rice

WHY THIS RECIPE WORKS

WHY THIS RECIPE WORKS

For our pressure-cooker take on classic chicken and rice, we used bone-in chicken breasts rather than boneless for better flavor and meat that stayed moist. Avoiding heavy, greasy rice was the biggest challenge. Browning the breasts before cooking them under pressure allowed us to keep the flavorful fond but render off and discard most of the fat before cooking. We also decreased the liquid in the standard 2:1 ratio of liquid to rice to account for the moisture released by the chicken and carrots that couldn't evaporate. Stirring the rice made the dish gluey, so we simply fluffed it with a fork when incorporating the peas, lemon juice, and parsley.

INGREDIENTS

- 4 (12-ounce) bone-in split chicken breasts, trimmed
  Salt and pepper
- 1 tablespoon vegetable oil
- 3 carrots, peeled and cut into ½-inch pieces
- 1 onion, chopped fine
- 1½ cups long-grain white rice
- 4 garlic cloves, minced
- 2 cups low-sodium chicken broth
- 1 cup frozen peas
- 3 tablespoons minced fresh parsley
- 2 teaspoons lemon juice

1. BUILD FLAVOR: Pat chicken dry with paper towels and season with salt and pepper. Heat oil in pressure-cooker

SERVES	TOTAL TIME
4	ABOUT 1 HOUR

PRESSURE LEVEL	RELEASE
HIGH	QUICK

15 MINUTES
UNDER PRESSURE

pot over medium-high heat until just smoking. Brown chicken, skin side down, until golden, about 6 minutes; transfer to plate.

2. Pour off all but 1 tablespoon fat left in pot. Add carrots, onion, and ½ teaspoon salt and cook until vegetables are softened, about 5 minutes. Stir in rice and garlic and cook until fragrant, about 30 seconds. Stir in broth. Using wooden spoon, scrape up all browned bits stuck on bottom of pot and brush any rice off sides of pot. Nestle chicken, skin side up, firmly into rice.

3. HIGH PRESSURE FOR 15 MINUTES: Lock pressure-cooker lid in place and bring to high pressure over medium-high heat. As soon as pot reaches high pressure, reduce heat to medium low and cook for 15 minutes, adjusting heat as needed to maintain high pressure.

4. QUICK RELEASE PRESSURE: Remove pot from heat. Quick release pressure, then carefully remove lid, allowing steam to escape away from you.

5. BEFORE SERVING: Transfer chicken to serving dish and tent loosely with aluminum foil while finishing rice. Sprinkle peas, parsley, and lemon juice over rice, cover, and let stand until for 5 minutes. Fluff rice gently with fork and season with salt and pepper to taste. Serve with chicken.

MAKING CHICKEN AND RICE IN A PRESSURE COOKER

Browning the chicken before cooking it under pressure does two important things. First, it gives the broth a deeper, richer chicken flavor that then gets absorbed by the rice. Second, it gives the chicken a little color so that it looks more appealing when served.

Do not rinse the rice before adding it to the pot or else it will stick to the pot's bottom and may scorch during cooking. Stirring the rice into the pot before adding the broth is also important because the rice gets coated with a thin layer of oil that helps prevent clumping as it cooks.

After adding the broth to the pot, take your time scraping up all the browned bits off the pot's bottom; if you miss any, the cooked rice might stick during cooking. Also, scrape any grains of rice stuck to the sides of the pot back into the broth to ensure they cook through.

Once you release pressure, be gentle with the rice to ensure it doesn't turn gummy. Just sprinkle the peas, parsley, and lemon juice over the top of the rice, cover the pot, let the rice steam and the peas cook through off the heat, then gently fluff the flavorings into the cooked rice with a fork.

TROUBLESHOOTING

Can I use boneless breasts?	No, you can't, because they would cook through long before the rice is done.
Do I need to alter the recipe for a 6-quart electric pressure cooker?	Yes, brown the chicken in 2 batches in step 1, using additional oil as needed. Quick release the pressure immediately after the pressurized cooking time; do not let the cooker switch to the warm setting.

VARIATIONS

Easy Spanish-Style Chicken and Rice

Omit carrots. Add 4 ounces chorizo, cut into ¼-inch pieces, 1 finely chopped red bell pepper, and ⅛ teaspoon crumbled saffron threads to pot with onion and salt in step 2.

Easy Chicken and Rice with Spinach and Feta

Omit carrots, parsley, and peas. Add 4 ounces coarsely chopped baby spinach and 2 ounces crumbled feta with lemon juice in step 5.

Chicken Curry with Chickpeas and Cauliflower

✔ WHY THIS RECIPE WORKS

Curries are especially well suited to cooking under pressure since pressure cookers amplify the flavor of spices and seasonings. We started by browning half of the chicken to create some fond, then sautéed the spices along with onion and tomato paste to help develop their flavor. We rounded out the curry's base with some chicken broth. Nutty chickpeas and cauliflower worked well here, absorbing the flavors of the curry and complementing the mild chicken. The cooking time of the chicken was too short to allow for cooking dried chickpeas at the same time, so we used canned. We added both ingredients after cooking the chicken under pressure to more easily monitor their doneness and ensure they didn't blow out or become mushy. Some coconut milk (also added at the end for fresher flavor) completed our curry with a touch of richness.

INGREDIENTS

- 8 (5- to 7-ounce) bone-in chicken thighs, trimmed
  Salt and pepper
- 1 tablespoon vegetable oil
- 2 onions, chopped fine
- 6 garlic cloves, minced
- 1 tablespoon curry powder
- 2 teaspoons grated fresh ginger
- 1 tablespoon tomato paste
- 1 teaspoon garam masala
- 1 cup low-sodium chicken broth
- ½ head cauliflower (1 pound), cored and cut into 1-inch florets

SERVES	TOTAL TIME
4	ABOUT 1¼ HOURS

PRESSURE LEVEL	RELEASE
HIGH	QUICK

20 MINUTES
UNDER PRESSURE

1 **(14-ounce) can chickpeas,
   rinsed**
½ **cup coconut milk**
½ **cup frozen peas**
¼ **cup minced fresh cilantro**

1. BUILD FLAVOR: Pat chicken dry with paper towels and season with salt and pepper. Heat oil in pressure-cooker pot over medium-high heat until just smoking. Brown half of thighs, skin side down, until golden, about 6 minutes; transfer to plate. Remove and discard skin from browned and unbrowned thighs. Pour off all but 1 tablespoon fat from pot.

2. Add onions to fat left in pot and cook over medium heat until softened, about 5 minutes. Stir in garlic, curry powder, ginger, tomato paste, and garam masala and cook until fragrant, about 1 minute. Stir in broth. Using wooden spoon, scrape up all browned bits stuck on bottom of pot. Nestle chicken with any accumulated juices into pot.

3. HIGH PRESSURE FOR 20 MINUTES: Lock pressure-cooker lid in place and bring to high pressure over medium-high heat. As soon as pot reaches high pressure, reduce heat to medium-low and cook for 20 minutes, adjusting heat as needed to maintain high pressure.

4. QUICK RELEASE PRESSURE: Remove pot from heat. Quick release pressure, then carefully remove lid, allowing steam to escape away from you.

MAKING CHICKEN CURRY IN A PRESSURE COOKER

Browning the chicken is crucial in order to develop a hearty flavor in the sauce. However, we found that browning just half the thighs gave the curry enough depth and saved us from browning two batches. Thighs are typically fairly fatty, so use a splatter screen for this step if necessary.

Even though using the pressure cooker is the ultimate method for maximizing the flavor of spices in a dish, we still start by sautéing them in the pot with a little oil (and the onions and garlic) before adding liquid. This step, referred to as "blooming" the spices, removes their raw edge.

Once the chicken is cooked, we remove it from the pot and add the cauliflower and chickpeas. Simmering them uncovered allows us to keep an eye on both ingredients and ensure they don't overcook. We also add the coconut milk after pressure is released to retain its fresh flavor.

TROUBLESHOOTING

Can I substitute bone-in chicken breasts here?	Yes, you can substitute 4 (12-ounce) bone-in chicken breasts for the thighs; decrease the pressurized cooking time to 15 minutes.
Does it matter which brand of curry powder I use and whether it is sweet or hot?	Yes, the brand of curry powder you use can have a big effect on the flavor of this dish. In the test kitchen, we use Penzeys Sweet Curry Powder. Or, for a spicier dish, you could substitute hot curry powder for all or a portion of the sweet curry powder.
Do I need to alter the recipe for a 6-quart electric pressure cooker?	Yes, quick release the pressure immediately after the pressurized cooking time; do not let the cooker switch to the warm setting. Use the browning (not the simmer) setting to simmer the cauliflower in step 5.

5. BEFORE SERVING: Transfer chicken to plate and tent loosely with aluminum foil. Bring sauce to simmer, stir in cauliflower, chickpeas, and coconut milk and cook until cauliflower is tender, about 15 minutes. Stir in peas and cook until heated through, about 2 minutes. Stir in cilantro and season with salt and pepper to taste. Off heat, return chicken to pot and let heat through, about 2 minutes. Serve.

Classic Smothered Chops with Onions and Bacon

WHY THIS RECIPE WORKS

The best smothered pork chops are fall-off-the-bone tender and covered with a deeply flavored caramelized onion gravy. A few tests proved that ¾-inch-thick blade-cut chops were crucial since they contain enough fat and connective tissue to keep the meat tender and moist. We started by cooking bacon in the pressure-cooker pot, and after setting the crisped pieces aside, we used some of the rendered fat to brown the chops and onions. Chicken broth plus flour gave us a gravy with the proper consistency, and garlic and thyme lent some depth. The gravy provided the moisture the chops needed to cook through under pressure, then we set the cooked chops aside, stirred some parsley into the sauce, and poured it over our chops. Topping it all off with the reserved bacon bits made a great smoky finish.

INGREDIENTS

- **6** slices bacon, cut into ½-inch pieces
- **4** (8- to 10-ounce) bone-in blade-cut pork chops, ¾ inch thick, trimmed
  Salt and pepper
- **2** onions, halved and sliced thin
- **2** garlic cloves, minced
- **1** teaspoon minced fresh thyme or ¼ teaspoon dried
- **2** tablespoons all-purpose flour
- **1¾** cups low-sodium chicken broth
- **1** tablespoon minced fresh parsley

SERVES	TOTAL TIME
4	ABOUT 1¼ HOURS

PRESSURE LEVEL	RELEASE
HIGH	NATURAL

10 MINUTES
UNDER PRESSURE

1. **BUILD FLAVOR:** Cook bacon in pressure-cooker pot over medium-high heat until crisp, about 5 minutes. Using slotted spoon, transfer bacon to paper towel–lined plate; reserve 3 tablespoons fat from pot.

2. Pat pork dry with paper towels. Cut 2 slits, about 2 inches apart, through outer layer of fat and silverskin on each chop; season with salt and pepper. Heat 1 tablespoon reserved bacon fat in now-empty pot over medium-high heat until just smoking. Brown half of chops on both sides, 6 to 8 minutes; transfer to plate. Repeat with 1 tablespoon bacon fat and remaining chops.

3. Add remaining 1 tablespoon bacon fat and onions to now-empty pot and cook over medium heat until softened and lightly browned, 5 to 7 minutes. Stir in garlic and thyme and cook until fragrant, about 30 seconds. Stir in flour and cook for 1 minute. Whisk in broth, smoothing out any lumps. Using wooden spoon, scrape up all browned bits stuck on bottom of pot. Nestle chops with any accumulated juices into pot.

TEST KITCHEN TIP PREVENTING CURLED PORK CHOPS

As pork chops cook, the fat and silverskin around the edges contracts and will cause the chops to bow, or curl. To prevent this and ensure better browning and more even cooking, cut slits in sides of each chop.

Using sharp knife, cut two slits, about 2 inches apart, into fat and silverskin of each chop.

TROUBLESHOOTING

Can I use boneless chops?	No, boneless chops will turn out dry and tough in this recipe.
I can't find blade chops; what can I substitute?	Very often, the chops cut from the shoulder end of the loin (aka blade chops) aren't labeled specifically as such. Just look for bone-in chops with a good streak of dark meat running through the center of the chop, or for chops with as much dark meat as possible.
Do I need to alter the recipe for a 6-quart electric pressure cooker?	Yes, turn the cooker off immediately after the pressurized cooking time and let the pressure release naturally for 15 minutes; do not let the cooker switch to the warm setting. Increase the simmering time to 15 minutes in step 6 and use the browning (not the simmer) setting.

4. **HIGH PRESSURE FOR 10 MINUTES:** Lock pressure-cooker lid in place and bring to high pressure over medium-high heat. As soon as pot reaches high pressure, reduce heat to medium-low and cook for 10 minutes, adjusting heat as needed to maintain high pressure.

5. **NATURALLY RELEASE PRESSURE:** Remove pot from heat and allow pressure to release naturally for 15 minutes. Quick release any remaining pressure, then carefully remove lid, allowing steam to escape away from you.

6. **BEFORE SERVING:** Transfer chops to serving dish, tent loosely with aluminum foil, and let rest while finishing sauce. Bring sauce to simmer and cook until thickened, about 5 minutes. Stir in parsley and season with salt and pepper to taste. Pour sauce over chops, sprinkle with bacon, and serve.

Pork Tenderloin with Apples and Cranberries

WHY THIS RECIPE WORKS

Cooking lean, thin pork tenderloins in a pressure cooker is tricky since they can overcook so quickly. After several tests, we found that even one minute of pressurized cooking followed by a 15-minute natural release turned out tenderloins that were overcooked. Switching to a quick release gave us slightly better control over the meat's doneness, but the dramatic change in pressure at the time of the release caused the meat to turn tough. In the end, we discovered perfectly cooked, juicy pork tenderloins required removing the pot from the heat as soon as high pressure was reached, then allowing the pressure to release naturally for 15 minutes. Pork and fruit are a natural, classic combination, so we included a mix of apples and dried cranberries in the pot. Seasoning the pork with some herbes de Provence ensured there was a savory flavor to balance the fruit's sweetness. We cut the apples into quarters to allow them to cook to the proper doneness in the same time as the pork, and it also kept the prep easy. Apple cider, brown sugar, and a tablespoon of butter to finish created the perfect accompanying sauce.

SERVES	TOTAL TIME	
4 TO 6	**ABOUT 45 MINUTES**	**LESS THAN 1 MINUTE**
PRESSURE LEVEL	RELEASE	
HIGH	**NATURAL**	**UNDER PRESSURE**

INGREDIENTS

2   **(12- to 16-ounce) pork tenderloins, trimmed**

2   **teaspoons dried herbes de Provence**
    Salt and pepper

2 tablespoons vegetable oil
1 tablespoon all-purpose flour
1 cup apple cider
1½ pounds Granny Smith apples, peeled, cored, and quartered
½ cup dried cranberries
1 tablespoon packed brown sugar
1 tablespoon unsalted butter

1. BUILD FLAVOR: Pat pork dry with paper towels and season with herbes de Provence, salt, and pepper. Heat 1 tablespoon oil in pressure-cooker pot over medium-high heat until just smoking. Brown tenderloins on all sides, 6 to 8 minutes; transfer to plate.

2. Add flour and remaining 1 tablespoon oil to now-empty pot and cook over medium heat for 1 minute. Whisk in apple cider, smoothing out any lumps. Stir in apples, cranberries, and sugar. Using wooden spoon, scrape up all browned bits stuck on bottom of pot. Nestle tenderloins with any accumulated juices into pot.

3. HIGH PRESSURE THEN NATURALLY RELEASE PRESSURE: Lock pressure-cooker lid in place and bring to high pressure over medium-high heat. As soon as pot reaches high pressure, remove pot from heat and allow pressure to release naturally for 15 minutes. Quick release any remaining pressure, then carefully remove lid, allowing steam to escape away from you.

MAKING PORK TENDERLOIN IN A PRESSURE COOKER

The only prep the tenderloin requires before cooking is to remove the sinewy silverskin, which turns unpleasantly chewy once cooked. To remove it, slip a boning knife underneath the silverskin, angle the blade slightly upward, and use gentle back-and-forth motion to remove it from the tenderloin.

Since this cut of meat is so small and lean, it doesn't cook for even a minute, but we still add a full cup of liquid to the pot for cooking. The apple cider ensures the meat stays juicy and is infused with flavor. It also forms the foundation for the sauce.

Once the pressure has been released, transfer the meat to a carving board and tent it with aluminum foil to rest for a few minutes before slicing. During this resting time, the meat fibers will loosen and relax, allowing the juices to redistribute.

TROUBLESHOOTING

How do I know the tenderloin is cooked through?	We've never encountered underdone pork when preparing this recipe, but the center of the tenderloin should register 140 to 145 degrees before resting. If it is underdone, simmer it gently in the sauce over medium-low heat until it registers 140 to 145 degrees, adding water if the sauce becomes too thick.
Can I use other types of apples?	Yes, but the flavor of the sauce and the texture of the cooked apples will vary depending on the apples you choose. Apples that turn very soft when cooked, such as Red Delicious and McIntosh, may turn into applesauce.
Do I need to alter the recipe for a 6-quart electric pressure cooker?	Yes, bring the pot to low pressure (not high) in step 3, then immediately turn the cooker off and let the pressure release naturally for 15 minutes; do not let the cooker switch to the warm setting. Use the browning (not the simmer) setting to simmer the apple mixture in step 4.

4. BEFORE SERVING: Transfer tenderloins to carving board, tent loosely with aluminum foil, and let rest while finishing sauce. Bring apple mixture to gentle simmer, stir in butter, and season with salt and pepper to taste. Slice pork and serve with apple mixture.

Shredded Pork Soft Tacos

9/2019 Delicious and easy used 3 pound pork butt Add garlic

✔ **WHY THIS RECIPE WORKS**

Weeknight tacos are usually limited to quick-cooking fillings like ground beef, but the pressure cooker makes pork butt, which would take hours in the oven, an option. We combined pork with orange juice, chipotle, cumin, and oregano. After 25 minutes under pressure, the pork was fall-apart tender and flavorful. Then we reduced the braising liquid for more depth. Refining the liquid's flavors with a little sugar and some lime juice at the end completed the dish. Pork butt roast is often labeled Boston butt in the supermarket.

INGREDIENTS

- 1 (4-pound) boneless pork butt roast, trimmed and cut into 2-inch pieces
- ½ cup water
- 1 onion, peeled and halved though root end, plus 1 onion chopped fine for serving
- 1 tablespoon minced canned chipotle chile in adobo sauce
- 1 tablespoon minced fresh oregano or 1 teaspoon dried
- 1 tablespoon sugar
- 1 teaspoon ground cumin
  Salt and pepper
- 2 bay leaves
- 1 orange, halved
- 2 tablespoons lime juice, plus lime wedges for serving
- 18 (6-inch) corn tortillas, warmed
  Fresh cilantro leaves
  Thinly sliced radishes

SERVES	TOTAL TIME
6	**ABOUT 1¼ HOURS**

PRESSURE LEVEL	RELEASE
HIGH	**NATURAL**

25 MINUTES
UNDER PRESSURE

1. HIGH PRESSURE FOR 25 MINUTES:
Combine pork, water, onion halves, chipotle, oregano, sugar, cumin, 1 teaspoon salt, ½ teaspoon pepper, and bay leaves in pressure-cooker pot. Juice orange into bowl and remove any seeds. Add juice from orange halves into pot, then add spent halves. Lock pressure-cooker lid in place and bring to high pressure over medium-high heat. As soon as pot reaches high pressure, reduce heat to medium-low and cook for 25 minutes, adjusting heat as needed to maintain high pressure.

2. NATURALLY RELEASE PRESSURE:
Remove pot from heat and allow pressure to release naturally for 15 minutes. Quick release any remaining pressure, then carefully remove lid, allowing steam to escape away from you.

3. BEFORE SERVING: Remove onion halves, orange halves, and bay leaves from cooking liquid. Using large spoon, skim excess fat from surface of sauce. Bring pork to simmer and cook, breaking up meat into bite-size pieces with wooden spoon, until cooking liquid has thickened, about 15 minutes. Stir in lime juice and season with salt and pepper to taste.

4. Serve pork with warm tortillas, chopped onion, cilantro, radishes, and lime wedges.

TEST KITCHEN TIP WARMING TORTILLAS

Warming the tortillas up before serving is crucial for both their flavor and texture. If your tortillas are very dry, pat each tortilla with a little water before warming them.

Toast tortillas, one at a time, directly on cooking grate over medium gas flame until slightly charred around edges, about 30 seconds per side. Or toast tortillas, one at a time, in dry skillet over medium-high heat until softened and speckled brown, 20 to 30 seconds per side. Once warmed, immediately wrap the tortillas in aluminum foil or a clean dish towel to keep them warm and soft until serving time.

TROUBLESHOOTING

Can I use another cut of pork?	Yes, you can substitute boneless country-style pork ribs; reduce the pressurized cooking time to 15 minutes. Note that this cut won't shred as well as the pork butt.
Do I need to alter the recipe for a 6-quart electric pressure cooker?	Yes, turn the cooker off immediately after the pressurized cooking time and let the pressure release naturally for 15 minutes; do not let the cooker switch to the warm setting. Increase the simmering time to 30 minutes in step 3 and use the browning (not the simmer) setting.

VARIATIONS

Shredded Beef Soft Tacos

Substitute 4 pounds boneless beef short ribs, well trimmed and cut into 2-inch pieces, for pork and increase pressurized cooking time to 35 minutes.

Shredded Chicken Soft Tacos

Substitute 4 (12-ounce) bone-in split chicken breasts, trimmed, for pork. Reduce pressurized cooking time to 15 minutes and use quick-release method.

After removing onion, orange, and bay leaves from pot in step 3, transfer chicken to cutting board, let cool slightly, and shred meat into bite-size pieces, discarding skin and bones. Meanwhile, simmer cooking liquid until thickened, about 10 minutes. Return shredded chicken to pot with lime juice and let heat through before serving.

Cuban-Style Beef with Onions and Bell Peppers

WHY THIS RECIPE WORKS

A Cuban-Creole dish by origin, *ropa vieja* is a simple preparation of shredded beef, peppers, and onions that has been braised in a deeply flavorful tomato sauce with olives, garlic, cumin, and oregano. To make it in our pressure cooker, we started with flank steak, which we found cooked to perfect tenderness more quickly than another popular choice, beef brisket, which also required a long sitting time before shredding. To cut down on prep, we browned only half of the meat, which supplied plenty of deep flavor for the sauce. With the reduced amount of evaporation that occurs in a pressure cooker, we found we needed to add less liquid to the pot at the outset than what you'd find in traditional recipes, and we also needed to simmer the sauce before serving to achieve the proper consistency. Though green pepper is standard in ropa vieja recipes, we also added a red pepper to offset the sometimes bitter taste that green peppers impart. A final splash of vinegar along with some sugar brightened the flavor and enhanced the sweetness of the peppers.

INGREDIENTS

- 2½ **pounds flank steak, trimmed and cut into 3-inch pieces**
- **Salt and pepper**
- 2 **tablespoons vegetable oil**
- 2 **onions, halved and sliced ½-inch thick**
- 3 **garlic cloves, minced**

SERVES	TOTAL TIME	
4 TO 6	**ABOUT 1½ HOURS**	**25 MINUTES**
PRESSURE LEVEL	RELEASE	
HIGH	**NATURAL**	**UNDER PRESSURE**

1 tablespoon minced fresh oregano or 1 teaspoon dried
1 teaspoon ground cumin
¼ teaspoon red pepper flakes
1 cup beef broth
1 (28-ounce) can crushed tomatoes
½ cup pitted green olives, halved
1 red bell pepper, stemmed, seeded, and cut into ¼-inch-wide strips
1 green bell pepper, stemmed, seeded, and cut into ¼-inch-wide strips
2 tablespoons minced fresh parsley
1 tablespoon white wine vinegar, plus extra as needed
1 teaspoon sugar, plus extra as needed

1. BUILD FLAVOR: Pat beef dry with paper towels and season with salt and pepper. Heat 1 tablespoon oil in pressure cooker pot over medium-high heat until just smoking. Brown half of meat on both sides, about 8 minutes; transfer to bowl.

2. Heat remaining 1 tablespoon oil in now-empty pot over medium heat until shimmering. Add onions and cook until softened, about 5 minutes. Stir in garlic, oregano, cumin, and pepper flakes and cook until fragrant, about 30 seconds. Stir in broth. Using wooden spoon, scrape up all browned bits stuck on bottom of pot. Stir in tomatoes, olives, browned beef with

MAKING CUBAN-STYLE BEEF IN A PRESSURE COOKER

Long shreds of beef are what give this dish its name (*ropa vieja*, or "old rope"). A flank steak cooked under pressure is the ideal choice, as the meat cooks through quickly and shreds easily into long pieces using two forks.

The texture of the bell pepper is another hallmark of this dish, and we found to avoid mushy strips it was best to simmer the pepper in the sauce while shredding the beef. This makes it easy to keep an eye on its texture and doneness.

TROUBLESHOOTING

Can I substitute another cut of meat for the flank steak?
We wouldn't recommend it. Beef brisket, the other possibility, takes much longer to cook through and requires a very long resting time.

Do I need to alter the recipe for a 6-quart electric pressure cooker?
Yes, turn the cooker off immediately after the pressurized cooking time and let the pressure release naturally for 15 minutes; do not let the cooker switch to the warm setting. Use the browning (not the simmer) setting to simmer the sauce in step 5.

any accumulated juices, and remaining unbrowned beef.

3. HIGH PRESSURE FOR 25 MINUTES: Lock pressure-cooker lid in place and bring to high pressure over medium-high heat. As soon as pot reaches high pressure, reduce heat to medium-low and cook for 25 minutes, adjusting heat as needed to maintain high pressure.

4. NATURALLY RELEASE PRESSURE: Remove pot from heat and allow pressure to release naturally for 15 minutes. Quick release any remaining pressure,

then carefully remove lid, allowing steam to escape away from you.

5. BEFORE SERVING: Transfer beef to cutting board, let cool slightly, then shred meat into bite-size pieces. Meanwhile, bring sauce to simmer, stir in bell peppers, and cook until tender, about 15 minutes. Stir in shredded beef, parsley, vinegar, and sugar. Season with salt, pepper, extra vinegar, and extra sugar to taste and serve.

Italian Meatloaf

WHY THIS RECIPE WORKS
Meatloaf typically takes about an hour and a half in the oven; since we'd already made meatballs in the pressure cooker (see page 60), we thought meatloaf was another good candidate. To start, we borrowed a technique we often use in the slow cooker: using an aluminum foil sling. The sling allowed us to form a meatloaf that held its shape and was easy to insert and remove from the pot. For a flavor boost, we swapped out the dairy product you'd find in a typical panade for marinara. This mixture not only ensured a tender meatloaf that held together, but it also gave the loaf some Italian flavor. Packing the mixture well ensured it didn't break apart under pressure. In less than 30 minutes of cooking time our meatloaf was done. For a topping, we layered over slices of another Italian favorite: provolone cheese. Our favorite brand of jarred marinara is Victoria Marinara Sauce.

INGREDIENTS
- ½ cup panko bread crumbs
- 2½ cups jarred marinara sauce
- 1½ pounds meatloaf mix
- 1 ounce Parmesan cheese, grated (½ cup)
- ¼ cup plus 1 tablespoon chopped fresh basil
- 1 large egg, lightly beaten
- ¼ teaspoon garlic powder
  Salt and pepper
- 6 slices (6 ounces) deli provolone cheese

SERVES	TOTAL TIME	
4	ABOUT 45 MINUTES	
PRESSURE LEVEL	RELEASE	
HIGH	QUICK	

25 MINUTES
UNDER PRESSURE

1. MAKE SLING AND SHAPE MEATLOAF:
Fold sheet of aluminum foil into 12 by 8-inch sling. Mash panko and ½ cup marinara to paste in medium bowl with fork. Gently mix in meatloaf mix, Parmesan, ¼ cup basil, egg, garlic powder, ¼ teaspoon salt, and ¼ teaspoon pepper with hands until thoroughly combined. Shape meat mixture into 8 by 4-inch loaf across center of foil sling.

2. Pour remaining 2 cups marinara sauce into pressure-cooker pot. Using sling, transfer meatloaf to pot and nestle into sauce.

3. HIGH PRESSURE FOR 25 MINUTES:
Lock pressure-cooker lid in place and bring to high pressure over medium-high heat. As soon as pot reaches high pressure, reduce heat to medium-low and cook for 25 minutes, adjusting heat as needed to maintain high pressure.

4. QUICK RELEASE PRESSURE: Remove pot from heat. Quick release pressure, then carefully remove lid, allowing steam to escape away from you.

5. BEFORE SERVING: Lay provolone over top of meatloaf, cover, and let sit until cheese is melted, about 5 minutes. Using sling, transfer meatloaf to serving platter. Using large spoon, skim excess fat from surface of sauce. Stir remaining 1 tablespoon basil into sauce and season with salt and pepper. Slice meatloaf and serve with sauce.

MAKING MEATLOAF IN A PRESSURE COOKER

For tenderness and a binder, most meatball and meatloaf recipes rely on a panade made by mixing bread crumbs with a dairy product, such as milk. Instead, we mash the crumbs with marinara. This not only takes care of the standard panade jobs but also gives the meatloaf a big boost in flavor.

To make it easy to get the meatloaf in and out of the pressure cooker, we use a foil sling. Make a sling that is 8 inches wide, then shape the meatloaf across the center of the sling into an 8-inch-long loaf. Be sure to pack the meat mixture well so it doesn't break apart under pressure.

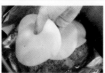

The downside to cooking meatloaf in the pressure cooker rather than the oven is that you simply can't make a loaf with a browned crust. To compensate, we lay slices of provolone over the top and let it melt into a cheesy topping using the residual heat after the pressure is released.

Once the cheese has melted, remove the meatloaf from the pot using the sling, and transfer it to a cutting board or platter. The meatloaf will slide off the sling easily with a spatula.

TROUBLESHOOTING

What if I can't find meatloaf mix?	You can substitute ¾ pound each 85 percent lean ground beef and ground pork.
What if my pressure cooker has a diameter less than 8 inches?	We made our sling to fit our Best Buy pressure cooker. If your pressure cooker has a smaller diameter at the base, this recipe will work fine; simply adjust the width of the sling accordingly to fit your cooker and shape the meatloaf to fit that smaller size. The cooking time will remain the same.
Do I need to alter the recipe for a 6-quart electric pressure cooker?	Yes, in addition to altering the meatloaf's size (see above), add 1 cup water to the pot with the tomato sauce in step 2. Quick release the pressure immediately after the pressurized cooking time; do not let the cooker switch to the warm setting. Before adding the basil in step 5, simmer the sauce for 10 minutes to thicken using the browning (not the simmer) setting.

BIG ROASTS AND FANCY MEALS

Classic Pot Roast and Potatoes

WHY THIS RECIPE WORKS

The typical 4-hour cooking time plus prep and rest make pot roast an unlikely candidate even on weekends for today's cooks. This pressure-cooker version makes it an easy weekend dinner. Adding potatoes seemed essential, and a few tricks guaranteed perfection. Adding them to the pot after the roast meant the slower-cooking meat was closest to the heat source. Large potatoes broke down during cooking, but potatoes measuring 1 to 3 inches held together. We flavored our braising liquid (beef broth) with tomato paste and dried porcini mushrooms (both boosters of meaty flavor) and used this braising liquid as our sauce.

INGREDIENTS

- 1 **(3- to 4-pound) boneless beef chuck-eye roast, trimmed**
  Salt and pepper
- 1 **tablespoon vegetable oil**
- 1 **onion, chopped fine**
- 2 **tablespoons tomato paste**
- ½ **ounce dried porcini mushrooms, rinsed and minced**
- 2 **cups beef broth**
- 2 **pounds small or medium Yukon Gold potatoes**

1. BUILD FLAVOR: Pat beef dry with paper towels, tie around circumference with kitchen twine, and season with salt and pepper. Heat oil in pressure-cooker pot over medium-high heat until

SERVES	TOTAL TIME
6	**ABOUT 2½ HOURS**

PRESSURE LEVEL	RELEASE
HIGH	**NATURAL**

1½ HOURS
UNDER PRESSURE

just smoking. Brown roast on all sides, 8 to 10 minutes; transfer to plate.

2. Add onion to fat left in pot and cook over medium-high heat until softened and browned, 5 to 7 minutes. Stir in tomato paste and porcini and cook, stirring constantly, until rust colored and fragrant, about 3 minutes. Stir in broth and simmer until slightly reduced, about 3 minutes. Using wooden spoon, scrape up all browned bits stuck on bottom of pot. Nestle browned beef with any accumulated juices in pot and place potatoes on top of meat.

3. HIGH PRESSURE FOR 1½ HOURS: Lock pressure-cooker lid in place and bring to high pressure over medium-high heat. As soon as pot reaches high pressure, reduce heat to medium-low and cook for 1½ hours, adjusting heat as needed to maintain high pressure.

4. NATURALLY RELEASE PRESSURE: Remove pot from heat and allow pressure to release naturally for 15 minutes. Quick release any remaining pressure, then carefully remove lid, allowing steam to escape away from you.

5. BEFORE SERVING: Transfer potatoes to serving dish. Transfer beef to carving board, tent loosely with aluminum foil, and let rest for 15 minutes. Using large spoon, skim excess fat from surface of sauce, then season with salt and pepper. Slice beef into thick pieces against grain. Serve with sauce and potatoes.

MAKING POT ROAST IN A PRESSURE COOKER

Our favorite cut for pot roast is a chuck-eye roast because it's well marbled and braises well. Most markets sell this roast with twine tied around the center, but if your roast is not tied, make sure to tie it around the middle once or twice before cooking.

Small potatoes 1 to 3 inches in diameter withstand the full 1½ hours of cooking time required for the meat surprisingly well and turn perfectly creamy and tender (larger potatoes will break apart). Arranging the potatoes on top of the roast ensures they cook through at the same time.

To remove the roast from the pot, use a spatula and tongs and transfer the roast to your carving board. Let the beef rest for 15 minutes before removing the twine and slicing it into pieces. Note that the meat will be extremely tender and begin to shred apart at the edges as you slice it.

TROUBLESHOOTING

Can I use another cut of meat instead of chuck roast?	We wouldn't recommend it. Although you may see other cuts, such as bottom or rump roasts, labeled as "pot roast" at the market, we've found they turn out tough and chewy once cooked.
Can I use a larger roast?	If you have an 8-quart pressure cooker, you can fit up to a 6-pound chuck-eye roast in the pot. For roasts that weigh between 4½ and 6 pounds, increase the pressurized cooking time to 2 hours. Also, a larger roast may render extra fat into the sauce; consider using a fat separator to help remove it before serving.
Do I need to alter the recipe for a 6-quart electric pressure cooker?	Yes, turn the cooker off immediately after the pressurized cooking time and let the pressure release naturally for 15 minutes; do not let the cooker switch to the warm setting.

Weeknight Pot Roast and Potatoes

✓ WHY THIS RECIPE WORKS

After developing a classic pot roast recipe (see page 96), we wondered if there was a way to speed things up even further to get a pot roast supper on the table in an hour. We started by slicing our chuck-eye roast, a step that we discovered cut the under-pressure cooking time by two-thirds and gave us portioned pieces of meat ready to serve. In lieu of a broth-based braising liquid that required chopping onions and garlic plus a mix of spices or herbs, we turned to condensed French onion soup. This single convenience product, plus dried porcini mushrooms, saved us shopping and prep time and created a beefy braising liquid with built-in aromatics. Plus, its condensed state meant that the sauce wouldn't get watered down once the meat began to release its juices. The finished jus has great body and complex flavor—you'd never guess it wasn't made from scratch. Finally, to make a meal, we arranged potatoes on top of the meat before cooking it. We prefer to use Yukon Gold potatoes measuring 1 to 3 inches in diameter in this recipe; do not substitute larger potatoes, or they will bust apart when cooked under pressure.

SERVES	TOTAL TIME	
4 TO 6	**ABOUT 1 HOUR**	**30**
PRESSURE LEVEL	RELEASE	**MINUTES**
HIGH	**NATURAL**	**UNDER PRESSURE**

INGREDIENTS

- 1 **(10.5-ounce) can condensed French onion soup**
- 2 **tablespoons tomato paste**
- ½ **ounce dried porcini mushrooms, rinsed and minced**
- 1 **(2½- to 3-pound) boneless beef chuck-eye roast, trimmed and cut across grain into 1-inch slices**
- 2 **pounds small or medium Yukon Gold potatoes**

1. HIGH PRESSURE FOR 30 MINUTES: Whisk soup, tomato paste, and porcini together in pressure-cooker pot, then lay sliced meat over top. Place potatoes on top of meat. Lock pressure-cooker lid in place and bring to high pressure over medium-high heat. As soon as pot reaches high pressure, reduce heat to medium-low and cook for 30 minutes, adjusting heat as needed to maintain high pressure.

2. NATURALLY RELEASE PRESSURE: Remove pot from heat and allow pressure to release naturally for 15 minutes. Quick release any remaining pressure, then carefully remove lid, allowing steam to escape away from you.

3. BEFORE SERVING: Transfer meat and potatoes to platter. Using large spoon, skim excess fat from surface of sauce and serve meat and potatoes with sauce.

MAKING WEEKNIGHT POT ROAST IN A PRESSURE COOKER

To cook an entire chuck-eye roast in less than an hour, we cut up the roast into 1-inch pieces that not only cooked through quickly but also were conveniently portioned, making serving easy. If the roast is very fatty, trim away excess fat before slicing it into portions.

In lieu of a broth-based braising liquid plus aromatics, we found a can of condensed French onion soup saved us shopping and prep time and offered just the right flavor. Plus, it didn't get overly watered down during cooking once the meat released its juices.

As with most larger cuts of meat, we use a natural release in this recipe. This roast is so fall-apart tender that the force of a quick release would actually cause the roast to break down into unappealing pieces.

The trick to getting the ultra-tender meat slices out of the pressure cooker is to use a spatula instead of tongs. The slices are delicate and prone to falling apart, so a gentle touch with a long, thin spatula is key.

TROUBLESHOOTING

Can I substitute other types of potatoes here?
Yes, small red or white potatoes can be substituted for the Yukon Golds; just make sure they are no larger than 3 inches in diameter.

Can I use a larger roast?
Yes, you can fit up to a 4½-pound chuck roast, sliced into 1-inch-thick pieces, in the pot. For roasts that weigh between 3½ and 4½ pounds, increase the pressurized cooking time to 40 minutes.

Do I need to alter the recipe for a 6-quart electric pressure cooker?
Yes, add 1 cup low-sodium chicken broth to the pot with soup, tomato paste, and porcini in step 1. Turn the cooker off immediately after the pressurized cooking time and let the pressure release naturally for 15 minutes; do not let the cooker switch to the warm setting. Before serving, simmer the sauce for 10 minutes to thicken using the browning (not the simmer) setting.

Sirloin Beef Roast with Mushroom Sauce

WHY THIS RECIPE WORKS

Turning an inexpensive cut of beef into a tender, rosy roast in the oven is an hour-long affair just for the cooking time. With our pressure cooker, a medium-rare roast was cooked through in just 20 minutes. Browning the roast was a good start for building a flavorful braising liquid (and eventual sauce). Once we'd set the roast aside, we sautéed onion and mushrooms; tomato paste, garlic, white wine, and chicken broth rounded the flavors out. Using a natural release ensured our roast came out ultratender. Once we'd set the meat aside to rest, we stirred in some cognac and simmered the liquid to reduce it to the right consistency. Butter and fresh parsley to finish gave the sauce color and richness, perfect for serving over thin slices of the roast.

INGREDIENTS

- 1 (3-pound) top sirloin beef roast, trimmed
  Salt and pepper
- 2 tablespoons vegetable oil
- 1 onion, chopped fine
- 6 ounces cremini mushrooms, trimmed and sliced thin
- 1 tablespoon tomato paste
- 3 garlic cloves, minced
- ¼ cup dry white wine
- 1½ cups low-sodium chicken broth
- 2 tablespoons cognac
- 1 tablespoon unsalted butter
- 2 tablespoons minced fresh parsley

SERVES	TOTAL TIME
6	ABOUT 1¼ HOURS

PRESSURE LEVEL	RELEASE
HIGH	NATURAL

20 MINUTES
UNDER PRESSURE

1. BUILD FLAVOR: Pat roast dry with paper towels and season with salt and pepper. Heat oil in pressure-cooker pot over medium-high heat until just smoking. Brown roast on all sides, 8 to 10 minutes; transfer to plate.

2. Add onion and mushrooms to fat left in pot and cook over medium-high heat until softened and browned, 5 to 7 minutes. Stir in tomato paste and garlic and cook, stirring constantly, until rust colored and fragrant, about 3 minutes. Stir in wine and simmer until slightly reduced, about 1 minute. Stir in broth. Using wooden spoon, scrape up all browned bits stuck on bottom of pot. Nestle browned roast with any accumulated juices into pot.

3. HIGH PRESSURE FOR 20 MINUTES: Lock pressure-cooker lid in place and bring to high pressure over medium-high heat. As soon as pot reaches high pressure, reduce heat to medium-low and cook for 20 minutes, adjusting heat as needed to maintain high pressure.

4. NATURALLY RELEASE PRESSURE: Remove pot from heat and allow pressure to release naturally for 15 minutes. Quick release any remaining pressure, then carefully remove lid, allowing steam to escape away from you.

5. BEFORE SERVING: Transfer roast to carving board, tent loosely with aluminum foil, and let rest for 15 minutes. Using large spoon, skim excess fat from

MAKING SIRLOIN ROAST IN A PRESSURE COOKER

There's not a lot of fat to trim off a sirloin roast, but you should remove any large pieces of visible fat. Be sure to remove any twine or elastic netting; we found we didn't need to tie the roast before cooking because it cooked evenly without it.

We take the roast out of the pot when it's slightly underdone since its internal temperature will continue to rise as it rests. In order to get the roast to perfect doneness, with a slightly rosy center, let the meat rest for 15 minutes after cooking it under pressure for 20 minutes and the natural release.

When serving this roast, it is important to slice it thin against the grain in order for the meat to taste tender (we're talking about ¼ of an inch). If the slices are cut too thick, the meat will have a chewy texture.

TROUBLESHOOTING

How do I know if the meat is cooked correctly?
After the natural release it should register about 105 degrees at the very center. If necessary, continue to simmer the roast gently until it reaches this temperature. After resting for 15 minutes, the temperature will climb to 120 to 125 degrees.

Can I use a larger or smaller roast?
Roasts smaller than 3 pounds do not work well in this recipe. Larger roasts (4 to 5 pounds) will work; increase the pressurized cooking time to 25 minutes. But note that by the time the center is medium-rare, the ends will be well done.

Could I substitute something else for the cognac?
Yes, brandy or Marsala can be substituted.

Do I need to alter the recipe for a 6-quart electric pressure cooker?
Yes, turn the cooker off immediately after the pressurized cooking time and let the pressure release naturally for 15 minutes; do not let the cooker switch to the warm setting.

surface of sauce. Stir in cognac. Bring to simmer over medium heat and cook until slightly thickened, about 10 minutes. Off heat, whisk in butter and parsley and season with salt and pepper to taste. Slice meat thin against grain and transfer to serving platter. Serve with sauce.

Corned Beef and Cabbage

WHY THIS RECIPE WORKS

Corned beef and cabbage makes its way to the dinner table (in this country, anyway) usually just once a year in celebration of St. Patrick's Day, and maybe for good reason. Aside from the 3-hour cooking time, the meat often comes out salty and dry and the vegetables mushy and bland. Using the stale spice packet that comes with the meat doesn't help. The pressure cooker cut the cooking time in half, and its moist cooking environment solved the dry meat issue. Making a braising liquid with chicken broth, peppercorns, allspice, bay leaves, and thyme infused the meat with flavor, and we used the liquid to moisten the meat at serving time. To avoid overcooked vegetables or the need to spend 20 minutes simmering them after the meat had cooked, we brought the pot up to pressure again and simply cooked the potatoes, carrots, and cabbage while the meat rested.

INGREDIENTS

1 **(3- to 4-pound) corned beef brisket, fat trimmed to ¼-inch and rinsed**

3 **cups low-sodium chicken broth**

3 **cups water**

2 **bay leaves**

3 **whole black peppercorns**

1 **tablespoon minced fresh thyme or 1 teaspoon dried**

½ **teaspoon whole allspice**

1½ **pounds small or medium red potatoes**

SERVES	TOTAL TIME
6 TO 8	**ABOUT 2¼ HOURS**

PRESSURE LEVEL	RELEASE
HIGH	**NATURAL**

1½
HOURS*

UNDER PRESSURE

*PLUS 12 MINUTES FOR VEGETABLES

10 carrots, peeled and cut into
   3-inch pieces
1 head green cabbage, cut into
   8 wedges

1. HIGH PRESSURE FOR 1½ HOURS: Place corned beef, broth, water, bay leaves, peppercorns, thyme, and allspice in pressure-cooker pot. Lock pressure-cooker lid in place and bring to high pressure over medium-high heat. As soon as pot reaches high pressure, reduce heat to medium-low and cook for 1½ hours, adjusting heat as needed to maintain high pressure.

2. NATURALLY RELEASE PRESSURE: Remove pot from heat and allow pressure to release naturally for 15 minutes. Quick release any remaining pressure, then carefully remove lid, allowing steam to escape away from you.

3. Transfer corned beef to carving board, tent loosely with aluminum foil, and let rest for 15 minutes. Using large spoon, skim excess fat from surface of cooking liquid.

4. HIGH PRESSURE FOR 12 MINUTES: Add potatoes, carrots, and cabbage to pot. Lock pressure-cooker lid in place, and bring to high pressure over medium-high heat. As soon as pot reaches high pressure, reduce heat to medium-low and cook for 12 minutes, adjusting heat as needed to maintain high pressure.

MAKING CORNED BEEF AND CABBAGE IN A PRESSURE COOKER

While browning meat is typically key for flavor, corned beef isn't browned before cooking. Instead, its unique flavor comes from the meat itself, which has been cured in a seasoned brine. As such, you can simply add the meat to the pot with the seasoning and liquid, lock on the lid, and cook.

To avoid overcooked vegetables, it's most efficient to cook the vegetables under pressure while the meat rests. It only takes 12 minutes for them to cook through, much faster than the time it would require to simmer them to the proper doneness.

When serving this roast, it is important to slice it thin against the grain in order for the meat to taste tender (we're talking about ¼ of an inch). If the slices are cut too thick, the meat will have a chewy texture.

TROUBLESHOOTING

Can I scale this recipe up to serve a crowd?
You can layer two (3- to 4-pound) briskets in the pot; the cooking time will remain the same. If one of the briskets is smaller, place it on the top. Also substitute water for the broth or else the meat will taste too salty. Double the vegetables, and cook them in two batches (the potatoes and carrots, then the cabbage) for 12 minutes each.

Do I need to alter the recipe for a 6-quart electric pressure cooker?
Yes. When cooking the corned beef, turn the cooker off immediately after the pressurized cooking time and let the pressure release naturally for 15 minutes; do not let the cooker switch to the warm setting. When cooking the vegetables, quick release the pressure immediately after the pressurized cooking time; do not let the cooker switch to the warm setting.

5. QUICK RELEASE PRESSURE: Remove pot from heat. Quick release pressure, then carefully remove lid, allowing steam to escape away from you.

6. BEFORE SERVING: Transfer vegetables to serving dish. Slice corned beef against grain into ¼-inch-thick slices and transfer to serving dish. Moisten corned beef and vegetables with cooking liquid as needed before serving.

Boeuf Bourguignon

SERVES	TOTAL TIME
6	ABOUT 1½ HOURS

PRESSURE LEVEL	RELEASE
HIGH	NATURAL

35 MINUTES
UNDER PRESSURE

✔ WHY THIS RECIPE WORKS

With tender hunks of beef in a red wine sauce, *boeuf bourguignon* is at once a rich, company-worthy meal and quintessential French comfort food. We swapped in easier-to-find bacon for the usual salt pork or fatback to add meaty depth, and richer, more-tender boneless short ribs were easier to prepare and cooked through more quickly than the usual chuck. Two cups of wine cut with beef broth created a balanced braising liquid and sauce. Because the pressure cooker concentrates flavors, a fruity, light-bodied red Burgundy or Pinot Noir was a must. While the mushrooms were fine under pressure, the delicate onions were better off sautéed separately.

INGREDIENTS

- 2 slices bacon, chopped fine
- 2 tablespoons tomato paste
- 1 tablespoon minced fresh thyme or 1 teaspoon dried
- ⅓ cup all-purpose flour
- 2 cups red Burgundy or Pinot Noir
- 1 cup beef broth
- 8 ounces cremini mushrooms, trimmed and sliced thin
- 2 bay leaves
- 3 pounds boneless beef short ribs, trimmed and cut into 2-inch pieces
  Salt and pepper
- 2 cups frozen pearl onions
- ½ cup water
- 1 tablespoon unsalted butter
- 1 tablespoon granulated sugar

2 tablespoons minced fresh
   parsley
1 tablespoon cognac

1. BUILD FLAVOR: Cook bacon in pressure-cooker pot over medium-high heat until browned and crisp, about 3 minutes. Using slotted spoon, transfer bacon to paper towel–lined plate. Add tomato paste and thyme to fat left in pot and cook until fragrant, about 30 seconds. Stir in flour and cook for 1 minute. Whisk in wine, smoothing out any lumps, and simmer until thickened, about 10 minutes. Stir in broth, mushrooms, and bay leaves. Using wooden spoon, scrape up all browned bits stuck on bottom of pot. Pat beef dry with paper towels, season with salt and pepper, and stir into pot.

2. HIGH PRESSURE FOR 35 MINUTES: Lock pressure-cooker lid in place and bring to high pressure over medium-high heat. As soon as pot reaches high pressure, reduce heat to medium-low and cook for 35 minutes, adjusting heat as needed to maintain high pressure.

3. NATURALLY RELEASE PRESSURE: Remove pot from heat and allow pressure to release naturally for 15 minutes. Quick release any remaining pressure, then carefully remove lid, allowing steam to escape away from you.

4. BEFORE SERVING: Bring pearl onions, water, butter, sugar, and ¼ teaspoon salt to boil in 12-inch nonstick skillet

MAKING BOEUF BOURGUIGNON IN A PRESSURE COOKER

We like using boneless short ribs in stews because they are easy to cut into evenly sized pieces, and they turn incredibly tender once cooked. The pieces of meat in boeuf bourguignon are traditionally cut a little larger than stew meat; we cut them into 2-inch pieces.

Cured pork is a key flavor in boeuf bourguignon. To keep things simple, we use bacon instead of the traditional salt pork or fatback. After browning the bacon to render the fat, we set it aside for sprinkling over each portion before serving. The bacon also leaves behind a fond in the pot.

Beef bourguignon relies on a good dose of wine. While a fine French Burgundy will give you an impressive, complexly flavored dish, a decent California Pinot Noir will perform perfectly well. We simmer it before bringing the pot up to pressure to round out the tannic edges and cook off alcohol.

Pearl onions and mushrooms are the classic vegetables. The mushrooms cook well under pressure, but the onions are too delicate. Thawing frozen pearl onions in a skillet with some butter and sugar is quick and easy and gives them a nice, caramelized flavor.

TROUBLESHOOTING

Do I need to alter the recipe for a 6-quart electric pressure cooker?
Yes, use the browning (not the simmer) setting to reduce the wine in step 1. Turn the cooker off immediately after the pressurized cooking time and let the pressure release naturally for 15 minutes; do not let the cooker switch to the warm setting. Before adding the onions, parsley, and cognac to the stew in step 5, simmer the stew for 15 minutes to thicken and drive off any remaining raw wine flavor using the browning (not the simmer) setting.

over high heat. Cover, reduce heat to medium-low, and simmer, shaking pan occasionally, until onions are tender, about 5 minutes. Uncover, increase heat to high, and simmer until all liquid evaporates and onions caramelize, about 3 minutes.

5. Remove and discard bay leaves from stew. Using large spoon, skim excess fat from surface of stew. Stir in onions, parsley, and cognac and season with salt and pepper to taste. Sprinkle individual portions with reserved bacon before serving.

Pomegranate-Braised Boneless Beef Short Ribs

✔ WHY THIS RECIPE WORKS

Nothing says special-occasion meal like a platter of rich, tender short ribs, but the traditional dish takes 5 hours to cook. We turned to the pressure cooker to get them on the table in a fraction of the time. To start, we chose boneless ribs over bone-in because they cook through more quickly and are easier to serve. We left the bacon in the pot during cooking so it could infuse the braising liquid with meaty flavor, then simply strained it out before serving. For our sauce, we decided on a fresh, modern spin, starting with a combination of pomegranate juice, orange zest and juice, thyme, garlic, and brown sugar to balance the tartness. As the short ribs and bacon cooked, they released juices that infused the sauce with just the right complementary meaty flavor. It was a little too thin and fatty, however, so we degreased the sauce, then cooked it down for 15 minutes to intensify the flavor. Waiting until this point to add balsamic vinegar kept its flavor rich and fresh, while cornstarch thickened the sauce up to the perfect consistency. A little butter gave this sauce just the right silkiness to complete our elegant dish.

SERVES	TOTAL TIME
6	ABOUT 1¼ HOURS

PRESSURE LEVEL	RELEASE
HIGH	NATURAL

35 MINUTES
UNDER PRESSURE

INGREDIENTS

- 2 slices bacon, chopped fine
- 1 onion, chopped fine
- 3 garlic cloves, minced
- 1½ cups unsweetened pomegranate juice
- 2 tablespoons brown sugar

4 **(2-inch) strips orange zest plus ½ cup juice**
2 **sprigs fresh thyme**
6 **(8-ounce) boneless beef short ribs, trimmed**
  Salt and pepper
2 **tablespoons balsamic vinegar**
1½ **tablespoons cornstarch**
1 **tablespoon unsalted butter**

1. BUILD FLAVOR: Cook bacon in pressure-cooker pot over medium-high heat until browned and crisp, about 3 minutes. Stir in onion and cook until softened, about 5 minutes. Stir in garlic and cook until fragrant, about 30 seconds. Stir in pomegranate juice, brown sugar, orange zest and juice, and thyme. Using wooden spoon, scrape up all browned bits stuck on bottom of pot. Pat short ribs dry with paper towels, season with salt and pepper, and nestle into pot.

2. HIGH PRESSURE FOR 35 MINUTES: Lock pressure-cooker lid in place and bring to high pressure over medium-high heat. As soon as pot reaches high pressure, reduce heat to medium-low and cook for 35 minutes, adjusting heat as needed to maintain high pressure.

3. NATURALLY RELEASE PRESSURE: Remove pot from heat and allow pressure to release naturally for 15 minutes. Quick release any remaining pressure, then carefully remove lid, allowing steam to escape away from you.

MAKING BRAISED SHORT RIBS IN A PRESSURE COOKER

Short ribs are notoriously fatty and need to be trimmed well before cooking. Using a sharp boning knife, trim away the large piece of fat on the top, and any fat on the bottom if necessary, of each rib.

We found pomegranate juice makes a great base for a richly flavored, elegant sauce for short ribs, so it serves as the necessary cooking liquid in this recipe. As the ribs braise, they infuse the juice with a meaty flavor that balances the juice's tart sweetness.

To prevent the sauce from being greasy, we strain and degrease the liquid before simmering it down into a sauce. Let the liquid sit in the fat separator for several minutes until the fat rises. Pour the liquid back into the pot and thicken it quickly with cornstarch into a dark, glossy sauce.

TROUBLESHOOTING

Can I substitute bone-in short ribs?	Yes, you can substitute 6 (12-ounce) bone-in English-style beef short ribs, well trimmed, for the boneless short ribs; increase the pressurized cooking time to 1½ hours.
What kind of pomegranate juice should I use?	Any kind of unsweetened pomegranate juice will work fine here; we've had good luck using POM Wonderful 100% Pomegranate Juice in the test kitchen. Stay away from sweetened juice or juice blends.
Do I need to alter the recipe for a 6-quart electric pressure cooker?	Yes, turn the cooker off immediately after the pressurized cooking time and let the pressure release naturally for 15 minutes; do not let the cooker switch to the warm setting. Increase the simmering time to 20 minutes in step 4, and use the browning (not the simmer) setting.

4. BEFORE SERVING: Transfer short ribs to platter, tent loosely with aluminum foil, and let rest while finishing sauce. Strain sauce into fat separator, let sit 5 minutes, then pour defatted sauce back into now-empty pot. Whisk vinegar and cornstarch together, then whisk into sauce and simmer over medium heat until thickened and measures 1½ cups, about 15 minutes. Off heat, whisk in butter and season with salt and pepper to taste. Serve sauce with ribs.

Asian-Style Boneless Beef Short Ribs

✅ **WHY THIS RECIPE WORKS**
One of the keys to pressure-cooker success is using enough moisture to cook the food through and keep the pan from scorching but also to provide good flavor that isn't too diluted. We decided an Asian-style sauce made with hoisin, soy sauce, and sherry would do a good job of accomplishing both goals for boneless beef short ribs. After 35 minutes under pressure, the meat was cooked through and had released its juices to create an intensely flavored sauce. It was more sauce than we would have gotten using a conventional stovetop or oven method since there was no evaporation from the pot, but we didn't mind having extra sauce on hand—mixed with some scallion greens and cilantro, it made an excellent match for a big bowl of steamed white rice.

INGREDIENTS

- 1 tablespoon vegetable oil
- 4 garlic cloves, minced
- 1 (2-inch) piece ginger, peeled, sliced into ¼-inch-thick rounds, and smashed
- ½ cup hoisin sauce
- 2 tablespoons soy sauce
- 2 tablespoons dry sherry
- 4 scallions, white parts chopped coarse, green parts sliced thin
- ¼ teaspoon cayenne pepper
- 6 (8-ounce) boneless beef short ribs, trimmed
- 2 tablespoons minced fresh cilantro

SERVES	TOTAL TIME
6	ABOUT 1 HOUR

PRESSURE LEVEL	RELEASE
HIGH	NATURAL

35 MINUTES
UNDER PRESSURE

1. BUILD FLAVOR: Cook oil, garlic, and ginger in pressure-cooker pot over medium-high heat until fragrant, about 1 minute. Stir in hoisin sauce, soy sauce, sherry, scallion whites, and cayenne, then add beef.

2. HIGH PRESSURE FOR 35 MINUTES: Lock pressure-cooker lid in place and bring to high pressure over medium-high heat. As soon as pot reaches high pressure, reduce heat to medium-low and cook for 35 minutes, adjusting heat as needed to maintain high pressure.

3. NATURALLY RELEASE PRESSURE: Remove pot from heat and allow pressure to release naturally for 15 minutes. Quick release any remaining pressure, then carefully remove lid, allowing steam to escape away from you.

4. BEFORE SERVING: Transfer short ribs to platter, tent loosely with aluminum foil, and let rest while finishing sauce. Strain sauce into fat separator, let sit 5 minutes, then pour defatted sauce into small bowl. Stir scallion greens and cilantro leaves into sauce and serve with ribs.

VARIATION

Asian-Style Short Ribs with Shiitakes

Add 1 pound shiitake mushrooms, stemmed and sliced, to pressure-cooker pot with beef in step 1. After straining sauce through fat separator in step 4, discard ginger pieces, then return strained mushrooms and defatted sauce to pressure-cooker pot and

TEST KITCHEN TIP PEELING AND SMASHING GINGER

We've found using a spoon to be an easy way to peel a knobby piece of ginger because you can easily maneuver around bumps. Adding a smashed piece of ginger at the beginning of cooking allows it to release its flavor, and the ginger is then easy to remove before serving.

1. Hold 2-inch piece of ginger firmly against cutting board and use edge of dinner spoon to scrape away skin.

2. Slice peeled ginger crosswise into ¼-inch-thick coins, then use corner of heavy pan (or mallet) to gently smash ginger.

TROUBLESHOOTING

Can I substitute bone-in short ribs?	Yes, substitute 6 (12-ounce) bone-in English-style beef short ribs, well trimmed, for the boneless ribs. Add ¾ cup of water to the pot with the beef in step 1 and increase the pressurized cooking time to 1½ hours. After defatting the sauce in step 4, simmer the sauce as needed to thicken before serving.
What if my short ribs don't seem tender after removing the lid?	If your short ribs don't look quite done after the 35-minute pressurized cooking time, gently simmer them in the sauce until they are done. If the sauce thickens too much, add water as needed.
Do I need to alter the recipe for a 6-quart electric pressure cooker?	Yes, turn the cooker off immediately after the pressurized cooking time and let the pressure release naturally for 15 minutes; do not let the cooker switch to the warm setting.

simmer gently as needed to thicken. Stir in 1 tablespoon Asian chili-garlic sauce with scallion greens and cilantro.

Osso Buco

WHY THIS RECIPE WORKS

A favorite special-occasion restaurant meal, osso buco features veal shanks braised in a flavorful cooking liquid of wine, broth, and tomatoes, garnished with a bright gremolata (a mixture of parsley, lemon zest, and garlic). When building our wine-and-broth braising liquid, we found several tablespoons of flour were essential to ensure it cooked down to the right consistency after releasing pressure. While the shanks rested, we reduced the sauce until it had a rich demi-glace consistency. The easy-to-prep gremolata lent just the necessary brightness to the rich dish. Serve with polenta, mashed potatoes, or risotto.

INGREDIENTS

- 6 (8- to 10-ounce) osso buco–style veal shanks, 1½ inches thick
  Salt and pepper
- 2 tablespoons vegetable oil
- 2 onions, chopped
- 2 carrots, peeled and chopped
- 9 garlic cloves, minced
- 2 tablespoons tomato paste
- 3 tablespoons all-purpose flour
- ½ cup dry white wine
- 2 cups beef broth
- 1 (14.5-ounce) can diced tomatoes, drained
- 2 bay leaves
- ¼ cup chopped fresh parsley
- 2 teaspoons grated orange zest

SERVES	TOTAL TIME
6	ABOUT 2¼ HOUR

PRESSURE LEVEL	RELEASE
HIGH	NATURAL

1 HOUR
UNDER PRESSURE

1. BUILD FLAVOR: Pat shanks dry with paper towels, tie each around circumference with kitchen twine, and season with salt and pepper. Heat 1 tablespoon oil in pressure-cooker pot over medium-high heat until just smoking. Brown half of shanks on one side, about 5 minutes; transfer to large plate. Repeat with remaining 1 tablespoon oil and remaining shanks; transfer to plate.

2. Add onions and carrots to fat left in pot and cook until onions are softened, about 5 minutes. Stir in two-thirds of garlic, then tomato paste, and cook until fragrant, about 1 minute. Stir in flour and cook for 1 minute. Whisk in wine, smoothing out any lumps, and cook until slightly reduced, about 1 minute. Stir in broth, tomatoes, and bay leaves. Using wooden spoon, scrape up all browned bits stuck on bottom of pot. Nestle browned shanks with any accumulated juices in pot.

3. HIGH PRESSURE FOR 1 HOUR: Lock pressure-cooker lid in place and bring to high pressure over medium-high heat. As soon as pot reaches high pressure, reduce heat to medium-low and cook for 1 hour, adjusting heat as needed to maintain high pressure.

4. NATURALLY RELEASE PRESSURE: Remove pot from heat and allow pressure to release naturally for 15 minutes. Quick release any remaining pressure, then carefully remove lid, allowing steam to escape away from you.

MAKING OSSO BUCO IN A PRESSURE COOKER

To keep the meat attached to the bone during cooking, you need to tie each shank tightly around the circumference. If you skip this step, the bones and meat will be separate in the pot.

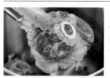
Browning the shanks creates a flavorful fond for the sauce and helps these big, bone-in pieces of meat look good for serving. But to save time and prevent the fond from burning, we brown only one side of each shank.

The gremolata is a traditional accompaniment to osso buco, and its bright, fresh, slightly spicy flavor is a welcome counterpoint to the rich sauce. Stir some of the gremolata into the sauce and sprinkle the rest over each shank before serving.

TROUBLESHOOTING

The meat on the raw shanks feels loose and pulls away from the bone easily; is this a problem?	It can be, so it's important to tie them up securely before cooking; otherwise they'll disintegrate under pressure. After tying them once around the circumference, also tie them around the top and sides (like a present) until they feel compact.
Do I need to alter the recipe for a 6-quart electric pressure cooker?	Yes, turn the cooker off immediately after the pressurized cooking time and let the pressure release naturally for 15 minutes; do not let the cooker switch to the warm setting. Increase the simmering time to 25 minutes in step 5, and use the browning (not the simmer) setting.

5. BEFORE SERVING: Transfer shanks to serving dish, tent loosely with aluminum foil, and let rest for 15 minutes. Bring sauce to simmer over medium-high heat and cook until slightly thickened, about 15 minutes. Strain sauce into fat separator, let sit 5 minutes, then pour defatted sauce back into now-empty pot.

6. To make gremolata, combine parsley, remaining garlic, and orange zest in bowl. Gently reheat sauce over medium heat until hot and season sauce with salt and pepper to taste. Off heat, stir in half of gremolata and let stand for 5 minutes. Remove twine from shanks, spoon sauce over top, and sprinkle with remaining gremolata as desired before serving.

Whole Chicken with Rosemary and Lemon Sauce

WHY THIS RECIPE WORKS

Getting a juicy whole bird with a richly flavored sauce in a pressure cooker required just a few key steps. Browning the skin created fond that lent the sauce and the chicken flavor, and placing the bird in the pot breast side up meant the slower-cooking dark meat was on the pot's bottom and got a jump start over the breast meat. After browning, we sautéed aromatics, then stirred in flour and deglazed the pot with wine. At this point the sauce was overly thick, but as the chicken cooked, it released juices that created a sauce that was flavorful and the perfect consistency.

INGREDIENTS

- 1 (4-pound) whole chicken, giblets discarded
  Salt and pepper
- 1 tablespoon vegetable oil
- 1 onion, chopped fine
- 3 garlic cloves, minced
- 2 teaspoons minced fresh rosemary or ½ teaspoon dried
- 2 tablespoons all-purpose flour
- ½ cup dry white wine
- ¾ cup low-sodium chicken broth
- 2 tablespoons unsalted butter
- 2 teaspoons lemon juice

SERVES	TOTAL TIME
4	ABOUT 1¼ HOURS

PRESSURE LEVEL	RELEASE
HIGH	QUICK

25 MINUTES
UNDER PRESSURE

1. BUILD FLAVOR: Pat chicken dry with paper towels and season with salt and pepper. Heat oil in pressure-cooker pot over medium-high heat until just smoking. Place chicken, breast side down, in pot and brown well, about 4 minutes. Using tongs, gently turn chicken over and brown back side of chicken well, about 4 minutes; transfer to plate. Pour off all but 1 tablespoon fat from pot.

2. Add onion to fat left in pot and cook over medium heat until softened, about 5 minutes. Stir in garlic and rosemary and cook until fragrant, about 30 seconds. Stir in flour and cook for 1 minute. Whisk in wine, scraping up any browned bits, and cook until slightly reduced, about 1 minute. Stir in broth. Place chicken, breast side up, in pot with any accumulated juices.

3. HIGH PRESSURE FOR 25 MINUTES: Lock pressure-cooker lid in place and bring to high pressure over medium-high heat. As soon as pot reaches high pressure, reduce heat to medium-low and cook for 25 minutes, adjusting heat as needed to maintain high pressure.

4. QUICK RELEASE PRESSURE: Remove pot from heat. Quick release pressure, then carefully remove lid, allowing steam to escape away from you.

5. BEFORE SERVING: Transfer chicken to carving board, tent loosely with aluminum foil, and let rest for 15 minutes. Using large spoon, skim excess fat from surface of sauce. Bring sauce to gentle simmer, whisk in butter and lemon juice, and season with salt and pepper to taste. Carve chicken, discarding skin if desired, and serve with gravy.

MAKING A WHOLE CHICKEN IN A PRESSURE COOKER

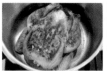
Even though browned skin can't stay crisp in the moist cooking environment of the pressure cooker, we still brown the skin to give the chicken visual appeal and to infuse the sauce with flavor.

Arranging the chicken in the pot breast side up is key to even cooking. Putting the slower-cooking dark meat in contact with the bottom of the pan allows it to finish cooking through at the same time the more delicate breast meat is done.

Just as with a roasted chicken, a whole chicken cooked under pressure should be rested for a few minutes before carving to allow the juices in the meat to redistribute.

While the chicken rests, we make the sauce. The liquid in the pot is infused with great meaty flavor from the juices of the chicken. After skimming off excess fat, all we need to do is whisk in butter, to give it a silky texture, plus a few teaspoons of lemon juice for some balancing brightness.

TROUBLESHOOTING

How do I know my chicken is cooked through?	After removing the lid, the breast should register 160 degrees and the thighs 175 degrees. If it isn't done, simmer the chicken until cooked through.
Can I use a larger chicken in this recipe?	If you have an 8-quart pressure cooker, you can fit up to a 5½-pound chicken in the pot. For chickens that weigh 5 pounds or more, increase the pressurized cooking time to 35 minutes.
Can I substitute chicken breasts?	Yes, you can substitute 4 (12-ounce) bone-in chicken breasts for the whole chicken; reduce the pressurized cooking time to 13 minutes.
Do I need to alter the recipe for a 6-quart electric pressure cooker?	Yes, quick release the pressure immediately after the pressurized cooking time; do not let the cooker switch to the warm setting. Before adding the butter and lemon to the sauce in step 5, simmer the sauce for 5 minutes to thicken using the browning (not the simmer) setting.

Turkey Breast and Gravy

SERVES	TOTAL TIME
6	**ABOUT 1½ HOURS**

PRESSURE LEVEL	RELEASE
HIGH	**QUICK**

35 MINUTES
UNDER PRESSURE

✓ WHY THIS RECIPE WORKS

With the help of a pressure cooker, we found we could make a juicy turkey breast and classic gravy in just 35 minutes of pressurized cooking time followed by a brief simmer. We browned the turkey breast to create some fond to flavor the sauce, then added our aromatics. We stuck with the classics: onion, carrot, garlic, and sage, plus white wine and chicken broth for the liquid. While the turkey rested, we cooked down the sauce and added butter and seasoning to finish.

INGREDIENTS

- 1 **(6-pound) whole bone-in turkey breast, trimmed**
  Salt and pepper
- 2 **tablespoons unsalted butter**
- 1 **onion, chopped fine**
- 1 **carrot, peeled and chopped coarse**
- 1 **garlic clove, peeled and smashed**
- 1½ **teaspoons dried sage**
- 3 **tablespoons all-purpose flour**
- ¼ **cup dry white wine**
- 2 **cups low-sodium chicken broth**
- 1 **bay leaf**

1. BUILD FLAVOR: Pat turkey breast dry with paper towels and season with salt and pepper. Melt 1 tablespoon butter in pressure-cooker pot over medium-high heat. Brown turkey breast, skin side down, about 5 minutes; transfer to plate.

2. Add onion and carrot to fat left in pot and cook over medium heat until softened, about 5 minutes. Stir in garlic and sage and cook until fragrant, about 30 seconds. Stir in flour and cook for 1 minute. Whisk in wine, smoothing out any lumps, and cook until slightly reduced, about 1 minute. Stir in broth and bay leaf. Using wooden spoon, scrape up all browned bits stuck on bottom of pot. Place turkey, breast side up, in pot with any accumulated juices.

3. HIGH PRESSURE FOR 35 MINUTES: Lock pressure-cooker lid in place and bring to high pressure over medium-high heat. As soon as pot reaches high pressure, reduce heat to medium-low and cook for 35 minutes, adjusting heat as needed to maintain high pressure.

4. QUICK RELEASE PRESSURE: Remove pot from heat. Quick release pressure, then carefully remove lid, allowing steam to escape away from you.

5. BEFORE SERVING: Transfer turkey breast to carving board, tent loosely with aluminum foil, and let rest for 15 minutes. Strain cooking liquid through fine-mesh strainer set over large bowl. Return liquid to pot and use large spoon to skim excess fat from surface. Bring liquid to simmer over medium heat and cook until thickened and measures 2 cups, about 15 minutes. Off heat, whisk in remaining 1 tablespoon butter and season with salt and pepper to taste. Carve turkey breast and serve with gravy.

TEST KITCHEN TIP PREPARING A TURKEY BREAST TO COOK UNDER PRESSURE

Before cooking the turkey under pressure, we trim the breast to ensure the gravy isn't greasy, and we brown the meat. While the moist cooking environment of the pressure cooker won't retain a crisped skin, browning builds up fond that adds critical flavor to the gravy, and it gives the turkey some visual appeal.

1. Trim excess skin and fat off turkey breast before cooking using kitchen shears.

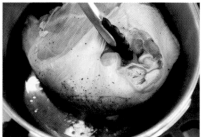

2. Pat turkey dry with paper towels, season with salt and pepper, and brown in 1 tablespoon melted butter over medium-high heat for about 5 minutes.

TROUBLESHOOTING

How do I know if the turkey is cooked through?	The turkey should register 160 degrees after removing the lid. If necessary, simmer the turkey breast gently until it reaches 160 degrees.
What if my gravy looks greasy?	Depending on the turkey and how well it's trimmed, the braising liquid might be overly greasy. If your braising liquid looks too greasy, simply pour it into a fat separator after straining in step 5; return degreased liquid to the pot and finish as directed.
Do I need to alter the recipe for a 6-quart stovetop or electric pressure cooker?	Yes, if the turkey breast's backbone is still intact (as pictured above in step 2), you will need to remove it using kitchen shears in order for the breast to fit into the pot; add the backbone to the pot, underneath the breast, to help flavor the gravy during cooking. For an electric cooker, quick release the pressure immediately after the pressurized cooking time; do not let the cooker switch to the warm setting.

INDOOR BARBECUE

Smoky Brisket

WHY THIS RECIPE WORKS

For a tender brisket, moving from the grill to the moist cooking environment of the pressure cooker proved ideal, plus we saved ourselves several hours of cooking time. We found that resting the brisket for just 1 hour was enough to turn the meat flavorful and sufficiently tender. To create a bold, smoky braising liquid and sauce, we sautéed onion, tomato paste, garlic, chipotle, and a few spices in the pot after browning the meat, then stirred in water, brown sugar, ketchup, and vinegar. Since we were translating the barbecue to the indoors, liquid smoke stood in for the charcoal-fired flavor with great success.

INGREDIENTS

1   (2- to 3-pound) beef brisket, preferably flat cut, fat trimmed to ¼ inch
     Salt and pepper
2   tablespoons vegetable oil
1   onion, chopped fine
2   tablespoons tomato paste
4   garlic cloves, minced
1   tablespoon minced canned chipotle chile in adobo sauce
1   tablespoon ground cumin
1   tablespoon paprika
1   tablespoon chili powder
½   cup water
½   cup packed dark brown sugar
¼   cup ketchup
1   tablespoon cider vinegar
½   teaspoon liquid smoke

SERVES	TOTAL TIME
4	ABOUT 3½ HOURS

PRESSURE LEVEL	RELEASE
HIGH	NATURAL

1½ HOURS
UNDER PRESSURE

1. BUILD FLAVOR: Pat brisket dry with paper towels and season with salt and pepper. Heat 1 tablespoon oil in pressure-cooker pot over medium-high heat until just smoking. Brown brisket on all sides, 8 to 10 minutes; transfer to plate.

2. Add onion and remaining 1 tablespoon oil to now-empty pot and cook over medium heat until softened, about 5 minutes. Stir in tomato paste, garlic, chipotle, cumin, paprika, and chili powder and cook until fragrant, about 30 seconds. Stir in water, sugar, ketchup, vinegar, and liquid smoke. Using wooden spoon, scrape up all browned bits stuck on bottom of pot. Nestle browned brisket with any accumulated juices into pot.

3. HIGH PRESSURE FOR 1½ HOURS: Lock pressure-cooker lid in place and bring to high pressure over medium-high heat. As soon as pot reaches high pressure, reduce heat to medium-low and cook for 1½ hours, adjusting heat as needed to maintain high pressure.

4. NATURALLY RELEASE PRESSURE: Remove pot from heat and allow pressure to release naturally for 15 minutes. Quick release any remaining pressure, then carefully remove lid, allowing steam to escape away from you.

MAKING SMOKY BRISKET IN A PRESSURE COOKER

Cooking brisket under pressure produces unbelievably tender, flavorful meat, but it's missing one key trait: that barbecued charcoal flavor. Liquid smoke infuses the meat (and sauce) with good grill-like flavor. It's very concentrated; don't be tempted to go overboard and add extra to the pot.

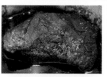

Brisket is a tough cut, and cooking it under pressure causes the meat's fibers to "seize" up—it would taste really tough if you ate it immediately. Resting the meat in the pot in its braising liquid after cooking gives it time to relax and turn more tender, plus the meat soaks up more flavor.

When slicing brisket, it is important to note which way the grain of the meat is running and to slice against the grain rather than with it. This keeps the meat from having a chewy texture. Pouring the reduced sauce over the slices allows them to soak up some moisture and flavor before serving.

TROUBLESHOOTING

Can I use a bigger or smaller brisket?	No, a larger brisket won't fit, and two smaller briskets won't cook evenly because of the small amount of liquid in the pot.
Do I need to alter the recipe for a 6-quart electric pressure cooker?	Yes, increase the amount of water to 1½ cups. Turn the cooker off immediately after the pressurized cooking time and let the pressure release naturally for 15 minutes; do not let the cooker switch to the warm setting. Increase the simmering time to 20 minutes in step 5, and use the browning (not the simmer) setting.

5. BEFORE SERVING: Let meat and sauce rest for 1 hour in pot. Transfer brisket to carving board, tent loosely with aluminum foil, and let rest while finishing sauce. Using large spoon, skim excess fat from surface of sauce. Bring sauce to simmer over medium-high heat and cook until thickened and measures 2½ cups, about 10 minutes. Season with salt and pepper to taste.

6. Slice brisket against grain into ¼-inch-thick pieces and lay in large casserole dish. Pour sauce over meat and serve. (Alternatively, cover dish tightly with foil and refrigerate overnight; reheat, covered, in 300-degree oven for 1 hour.)

Kalua-Style Pork

WHY THIS RECIPE WORKS

This Hawaiian-style barbecued pork traditionally involves slowly roasting suckling pig in a pit with hot rocks, banana leaves, and kiawe wood (the Hawaiian version of mesquite). Tasty, yes, but also a lot of work. We wanted pork with the same silky, tender texture and intense, earthy smokiness to come out of our pressure cooker. We rubbed a boneless pork butt with salt and pepper as well as green tea leaves to mimic the grassy flavor of the banana leaves. We then placed the roast in the pot along with some water and liquid smoke, which supplied the requisite smoky flavor. Cooking the roast under pressure produced juicy, tender meat that tasted like it had slowly cooked all day. While the pork rested, we made a quick pineapple salsa with scallions, jalapeño, and lime juice. Its bright, tangy flavor was the perfect balance to the richness of the pork. Don't trim the roast; the extra fat helps to ensure it remains moist. Pork butt roast is often labeled Boston butt in the supermarket.

INGREDIENTS

- **1** **tablespoon green tea leaves (about 2 bags)**
  Salt and pepper
- **1** **(4-pound) boneless pork butt roast**
- **2** **cups water**
- **½** **teaspoon liquid smoke**
- **2** **cups pineapple, cut into ¼-inch pieces**

SERVES	TOTAL TIME
6	**ABOUT 2¼ HOURS**

PRESSURE LEVEL	RELEASE
HIGH	**NATURAL**

1½ HOURS
UNDER PRESSURE

3 scallions, sliced thin

½ jalapeño chile, stemmed, seeded, and minced

4 teaspoons lime juice

1. BUILD FLAVOR: Combine tea leaves, 2 teaspoons salt, and ½ teaspoon pepper, then rub mixture evenly over pork. Combine water and liquid smoke in pressure-cooker pot and add spice-rubbed pork.

2. HIGH PRESSURE FOR 1½ HOURS: Lock pressure-cooker lid in place and bring to high pressure over medium-high heat. As soon as pot reaches high pressure, reduce heat to medium-low and cook for 1½ hours, adjusting heat as needed to maintain high pressure.

3. NATURALLY RELEASE PRESSURE: Remove pot from heat and allow pressure to release naturally for 15 minutes. Quick release any remaining pressure, then carefully remove lid, allowing steam to escape away from you.

4. BEFORE SERVING: Transfer pork to carving board, tent loosely with aluminum foil, and let rest for 15 minutes; discard braising liquid. Combine pineapple, scallions, jalapeño, and lime juice in bowl and mash gently with potato masher to break down some of the pineapple. Season with salt and pepper to taste. Slice pork into ½-inch-thick pieces and serve with pineapple salsa.

MAKING KALUA-STYLE PORK IN A PRESSURE COOKER

Traditional kalua pork wraps the roast in banana leaves, which we didn't want to track down or fuss with. We discovered that rubbing the meat with green tea leaves before cooking infuses the meat with a grassy, slightly bitter flavor that mimics banana leaf flavor.

For the cooking liquid, all we add is 2 cups of water plus liquid smoke (½ teaspoon goes a long way). The tea leaves on the meat mingle with the water, making a tea-infused liquid ideal for braising the meat.

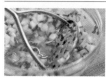

The tea-infused braising liquid is too bitter to use in a sauce—no surprise given the cooking time and fact that the pressure cooker concentrates flavors. So we serve the pork with a fresh, simple pineapple salsa. Mashing some pineapple helps release juice and gives the salsa a nice texture.

TROUBLESHOOTING

What kind of green tea should I use?	The brand or type of green tea doesn't matter, just don't use a green tea blended with other flavors, such as mint. If you buy bagged rather than loose tea, simply cut the bag open and measure out 1 tablespoon of tea.
I don't need to trim the pork?	No, we don't call for trimming the extra fat on the pork in this recipe for a reason. That extra fat is important to help the meat stay moist and tender during the cooking time. Most of the fat will render into the braising liquid during cooking (and that liquid will be discarded).
Can I substitute canned pineapple for the fresh?	We don't recommend using canned pineapple in this recipe because it's too mushy and flat in flavor, with a tinny aftertaste. However, the peeled and cored pineapple found in the produce section of the supermarket is just fine and will save you the prep work of peeling, coring, and cutting a whole pineapple.
Do I need to alter the recipe for a 6-quart electric pressure cooker?	Yes, turn the cooker off immediately after the pressurized cooking time and let the pressure release naturally for 15 minutes; do not let the cooker switch to the warm setting.

Pulled Pork

SERVES	TOTAL TIME
6 TO 8	**ABOUT 1½ HOURS**

PRESSURE LEVEL	RELEASE
HIGH	**NATURAL**

45 MINUTES
UNDER PRESSURE

✓ WHY THIS RECIPE WORKS

Requiring minutes of prep and ready in a fraction of the time of the grilled or oven-braised versions, pressure-cooker pulled pork is a sure win. We began by smothering a pork butt with a sweet-spicy dry rub, and cutting the meat into chunks created more surface area for the rub to penetrate. We often let meat sit for a few hours covered in the rub so it absorbs flavor, but the pressure cooker allowed us to skip that step since it amplifies seasonings so well. Cider vinegar, water, ketchup, and liquid smoke served as our braising liquid. After the pork was done, we defatted the cooking liquid and reduced it to 2 cups, then added more brown sugar and cider vinegar for a sauce with a clean finish. Pork butt roast is often labeled Boston butt in the supermarket.

INGREDIENTS

- 3 **tablespoons packed brown sugar, plus extra as needed**
- 2 **tablespoons paprika**
- 2 **tablespoons chili powder**
- 2 **teaspoons ground cumin**
  Salt and pepper
- 1 **(4-pound) boneless pork butt roast, trimmed and cut crosswise into 4 pieces**
- ¾ **cup cider vinegar, plus extra as needed**
- ½ **cup water**
- ½ **cup ketchup**
- ½ **teaspoon liquid smoke**
- 6–8 **hamburger buns**

1. BUILD FLAVOR: Combine sugar, paprika, chili powder, cumin, 1 teaspoon salt, and ½ teaspoon pepper, then rub mixture evenly over pork. Combine vinegar, water, ketchup, and liquid smoke in pressure-cooker pot. Nestle spice-rubbed pork into pot.

2. HIGH PRESSURE FOR 45 MINUTES: Lock pressure-cooker lid in place and bring to high pressure over medium-high heat. As soon as pot reaches high pressure, reduce heat to medium-low and cook for 45 minutes, adjusting heat as needed to maintain high pressure.

3. NATURALLY RELEASE PRESSURE: Remove pot from heat and allow pressure to release naturally for 15 minutes. Quick release any remaining pressure, then carefully remove lid, allowing steam to escape away from you.

4. BEFORE SERVING: Transfer pork to large bowl, let cool slightly, then shred into bite-size pieces, discarding any fat. Using large spoon, skim excess fat from surface of sauce. Bring sauce to simmer over medium-high heat and cook until thickened and measures 2 cups, 15 to 20 minutes. Season with salt, pepper, extra sugar, and extra vinegar to taste. Stir 1 cup sauce into shredded pork, then add extra sauce to taste. Serve shredded pork on buns with remaining sauce.

MAKING PULLED PORK IN A PRESSURE COOKER

To help the pork cook through more quickly and evenly, we cut the roast into four pieces after trimming away excess fat.

Rubbing the pieces of pork with a mixture of sugar, paprika, chili powder, cumin, salt, and pepper helps flavor both the pork and the sauce (which serves as the braising liquid) during cooking.

To shred the cooked pork into bite-size pieces, it's easiest to use two forks. Discard any pieces of fat that you come across as you are shredding.

Once the pork is shredded and the braising liquid has been simmered down into a sauce, we toss the pork with a good amount of the sauce to add flavor and moisture and serve extra sauce on the side.

TROUBLESHOOTING

Can I double this recipe?	No, but if you are using an 8-quart pot, you can increase all ingredients by 50 percent and increase the pressurized cooking time to 1¼ hours.
Do I need to alter the recipe for a 6-quart electric pressure cooker?	Yes, turn the cooker off immediately after the pressurized cooking time and let the pressure release naturally for 15 minutes; do not let the cooker switch to the warm setting. Use the browning (not the simmer) setting to simmer the sauce in step 4.

VARIATIONS

Shredded Barbecued Beef
Substitute 1 (4-pound) boneless beef chuck-eye roast, trimmed and sliced crosswise into 4 pieces, for pork butt roast.

Pulled Chicken
Substitute 4 pounds boneless, skinless chicken thighs, trimmed, for pork butt roast. Reduce pressurized cooking time to 25 minutes, and quick release pressure.

Barbecued Baby Back Ribs

SERVES
4 TO 6

TOTAL TIME
ABOUT 1½ HOURS

PRESSURE LEVEL
HIGH

RELEASE
NATURAL

30 MINUTES
UNDER PRESSURE

✓ WHY THIS RECIPE WORKS

We wanted to create a pressure-cooker version of barbecued ribs with the same fall-off-the-bone texture as their grill-roasted counterparts without the 4-hour-long cooking time. Covering the ribs with a dry rub of paprika, sugar, chili powder, cayenne, salt, and pepper ensured they would have good flavor, and cutting the ribs into two-rib sections made them easy to arrange in the pot. For the cooking liquid, we built the foundation for what would become our barbecue sauce: We sautéed onion and garlic, then stirred in ketchup, molasses, cider vinegar, and Dijon mustard. After arranging the ribs around the perimeter of the pressure-cooker pot, we poured some of the sauce over the tops of the ribs. As the ribs cooked, the sauce dripped down, slowly basting and flavoring the meat. After 30 minutes, we released the pressure, removed the ribs, and reduced the sauce to intensify its flavor and give it more body. For an authentic, lightly charred exterior, we arranged the ribs on a baking sheet and broiled them, brushing them with barbecue sauce every few minutes, until they were sticky and caramelized.

INGREDIENTS

- **3 tablespoons paprika**
- **2 tablespoons packed brown sugar**
- **2 teaspoons chili powder**
  Salt and pepper
- **¼ teaspoon cayenne pepper**

2   (1½- to 2-pound) racks baby
     back ribs, cut into 2-rib
     sections
1   tablespoon vegetable oil
1   onion, chopped fine
2   garlic cloves, minced
1   cup ketchup
½   cup water
¼   cup molasses
2   tablespoons cider vinegar
2   tablespoons Dijon mustard

1. BUILD FLAVOR: Combine paprika, sugar, chili powder, 1 teaspoon salt, 2 teaspoons pepper, and cayenne, then rub mixture evenly over ribs.

2. Heat oil in pressure-cooker pot over medium heat until shimmering. Add onion and cook until softened, about 5 minutes. Stir in garlic and cook until fragrant, about 30 seconds. Stir in ketchup, water, molasses, vinegar, and mustard. Measure out and reserve 1 cup sauce. Arrange ribs upright in pot with meaty sides facing outward, then pour reserved sauce over ribs.

3. HIGH PRESSURE FOR 30 MINUTES: Lock pressure-cooker lid in place and bring to high pressure over medium-high heat. As soon as pot reaches high pressure, reduce heat to medium-low and cook for 30 minutes, adjusting heat as needed to maintain high pressure.

4. NATURALLY RELEASE PRESSURE: Remove pot from heat and allow pressure to release naturally for 15 minutes.

MAKING BARBECUED RIBS IN A PRESSURE COOKER

Cutting each rack of ribs into 2-rib sections ensures all the ribs easily fit inside the pressure-cooker pot. This also makes things simpler when serving.

To tidily arrange the ribs in the pot and ensure even cooking, we arrange them upright around the pot's perimeter, sitting in some of the sauce, then pour more sauce over the tops of the ribs so that the sauce will baste them as they cook.

Because these ribs are cooked in the moist pressure-cooker environment, they're ultratender, but they don't develop any char like they would on the grill. To address this, we run the ribs under the broiler, basting them with sauce every few minutes, until they are charred and sticky.

TROUBLESHOOTING

Can I double this recipe?	No, two more racks of ribs won't fit in the pot, but if you are using an 8-quart pot, you can add one more rack of ribs. Increase all ingredients by 50 percent and increase the pressurized cooking time to 40 minutes.
Do I need to alter the recipe for a 6-quart electric pressure cooker?	Yes, turn the cooker off immediately after the pressurized cooking time and let the pressure release naturally for 15 minutes; do not let the cooker switch to the warm setting. Use the browning (not the simmer) setting to simmer the sauce in step 5.

Quick release any remaining pressure, then carefully remove lid, allowing steam to escape away from you.

5. BEFORE SERVING: Adjust oven rack 6 inches from broiler element and heat broiler. Place wire rack inside aluminum foil–lined rimmed baking sheet and spray with vegetable oil spray. Transfer ribs, meaty side up, to prepared baking sheet. Using large spoon, skim excess fat from surface of sauce. Bring sauce to simmer and cook until thickened and measures 2 cups, about 10 minutes. Brush ribs with some of sauce, then broil until browned and sticky, 10 to 15 minutes, flipping and brushing with additional sauce every few minutes. Serve ribs with remaining sauce.

Fiery Mustard Ribs

SERVES	TOTAL TIME
4 TO 6	**ABOUT 1¼ HOURS**

PRESSURE LEVEL	RELEASE
HIGH	**NATURAL**

30
MINUTES
UNDER PRESSURE

✔ WHY THIS RECIPE WORKS

For those who like it spicy (and a little bit messy), we set out to make a pressure-cooker ribs recipe that boasted not only tender, juicy ribs but also a sauce with a serious kick of heat. We already had the basics about preparing ribs in a pressure cooker figured out (see Barbecued Baby Back Ribs, page 124), so for this recipe, it was all about the sauce and spice. We started by tossing the ribs with chili powder, then we made a thick, spicy sauce beginning with a full cup of yellow mustard. Pickled banana peppers added tartness, and a habanero chile really brought home the heat. Stirring in some chili sauce (we used Heinz Chili Sauce) and brown sugar ensured the sauce wasn't one-sided, lending a necessary, balancing sweetness. We arranged the ribs in the pressure cooker with the sauce and poured more of the sauce on top of the ribs to baste them as they cooked. When they were done, we reduced the sauce to the right consistency. To give the ribs a charred exterior, after removing them from the pressure cooker we slathered them with the spicy sauce and put them under the broiler. After a few minutes under the intense heat and occasional basting with more of the sauce, we built up layers of flavor and gave our ribs the perfect sticky, caramelized exterior we were after.

INGREDIENTS

- **3 tablespoons chili powder**
- **2 (1½- to 2-pound) racks baby back ribs, cut into 2-rib sections**
- **1 cup water**
- **¼ cup jarred banana pepper rings, chopped fine, plus 2 tablespoons pickling liquid**
- **1 cup yellow mustard**
- **½ cup packed brown sugar**
- **½ cup chili sauce**
- **1 habanero chile, minced**

1. BUILD FLAVOR: Rub chili powder evenly over ribs. Add water to pressure-cooker pot, then arrange ribs upright in pot with meaty sides facing outward. Whisk banana peppers and pickling liquid, mustard, sugar, chili sauce, and habanero together, then pour mixture over ribs.

2. HIGH PRESSURE FOR 30 MINUTES: Lock pressure-cooker lid in place and bring to high pressure over medium-high heat. As soon as pot reaches high pressure, reduce heat to medium-low and cook for 30 minutes, adjusting heat as needed to maintain high pressure.

3. NATURALLY RELEASE PRESSURE: Remove pot from heat and allow pressure to release naturally for 15 minutes. Quick release any remaining pressure, then carefully remove lid, allowing steam to escape away from you.

TEST KITCHEN TIP WORKING WITH HABANEROS

Hotter than jalapeños and even serranos, habaneros are a very spicy chile that requires proper handling.

Wear gloves when working with habaneros to avoid direct contact with oils that supply heat. If you don't wear gloves, make absolutely sure to wash your hands thoroughly immediately after handling chile. Also wash your knife and cutting board well once you are finished prepping.

TROUBLESHOOTING

What is chili sauce, and is there an easy substitute?	Chili sauce is a lightly spiced condiment made with tomatoes, chiles or chili powder, onions, green peppers, vinegar, sugar, and spices. Don't confuse it with the chile sauces used in Asian cookery. For an easy substitute, combine ½ cup ketchup, 1 teaspoon Worcestershire sauce, ½ teaspoon hot sauce, and a pinch ground clove.
Can I double this recipe?	No, two more racks of ribs won't fit in the pot, but if you are using an 8-quart pot, you can add one more rack of ribs. Increase all ingredients by 50 percent and increase the pressurized cooking time to 40 minutes.
Do I need to alter the recipe for a 6-quart electric pressure cooker?	Yes, turn the cooker off immediately after the pressurized cooking time and let the pressure release naturally for 15 minutes; do not let the cooker switch to the warm setting. Use the browning (not the simmer) setting to simmer the sauce in step 4.

4. BEFORE SERVING: Adjust oven rack 6 inches from broiler element and heat broiler. Place wire rack inside aluminum foil–lined rimmed baking sheet and spray with vegetable oil spray. Transfer ribs, meaty side up, to prepared baking sheet. Using large spoon, skim excess fat from surface of sauce. Bring sauce to simmer and cook until thickened and measures 2 cups, about 10 minutes. Brush ribs with some of sauce, then broil until browned and sticky, 10 to 15 minutes, flipping and brushing with additional sauce every few minutes. Serve ribs with remaining sauce.

Easy Barbecued Wings

✔ **WHY THIS RECIPE WORKS**

Perfect wings should be moist and lacquered with a thick and sticky, sweet and tangy sauce. A cup of store-bought sauce was a good start, but adding paprika for flavor and color, brown sugar for balance, and cayenne for a bit of heat gave it a much-needed boost. Incorporating some water to thin out the sauce was a must to prevent scorching. Once the wings were cooked, we reduced the sauce to intensify the flavor and give it more body. While the sauce reduced, we started the wings under the broiler to char their exterior. Halfway through, the sauce was ready so we brushed some over the wings and kept on broiling until they were sticky, saucy, and perfectly caramelized. The test kitchen's favorite brand of barbecue sauce is Bull's-Eye Original.

INGREDIENTS

- 4 **pounds chicken wings, halved at joint and wingtips removed, trimmed**
- 1 **cup barbecue sauce**
- 1 **cup water**
- 1½ **tablespoons paprika**
- 1 **tablespoon packed brown sugar**
- 1 **teaspoon pepper**
- ½ **teaspoon salt**
  Pinch cayenne pepper

SERVES	TOTAL TIME
4 TO 6	**ABOUT 45 MINUTES**

PRESSURE LEVEL	RELEASE
HIGH	**QUICK**

10 MINUTES
UNDER PRESSURE

1. HIGH PRESSURE FOR 10 MINUTES: Place wings in pot. Combine barbecue sauce, water, paprika, sugar, pepper, salt, and cayenne, then pour over wings.

Lock pressure-cooker lid in place and bring to high pressure over medium-high heat. As soon as pot reaches high pressure, reduce heat to medium-low and cook for 10 minutes, adjusting heat as needed to maintain high pressure.

2. QUICK RELEASE PRESSURE: Remove pot from heat. Quick release pressure, then carefully remove lid, allowing steam to escape away from you.

3. BEFORE SERVING: Adjust oven rack 6 inches from broiler element and heat broiler. Place wire rack inside aluminum foil–lined rimmed baking sheet and spray with vegetable oil spray. Transfer wings to prepared baking sheet and broil until lightly charred and crisp, about 10 minutes, flipping halfway through cooking. Meanwhile, bring sauce left in pot to simmer and cook until thickened, about 10 minutes.

4. Brush wings with some of reduced sauce and continue to broil until wings are browned and sticky, 10 to 15 minutes, flipping and brushing wings with more sauce halfway through cooking. Serve with remaining sauce.

VARIATIONS

Easy Asian-Style Wings
Combine 1 cup hoisin sauce, 1 cup water, 2 tablespoons rice vinegar, 1 tablespoon Sriracha sauce, and ½ teaspoon salt; substitute this mixture for barbecue sauce mixture in step 1. Stir 1 tablespoon rice vinegar into sauce after thickening in step 3.

Easy Peach-Bourbon Wings
Combine 1 cup peach preserves, 1 cup water, ¼ cup bourbon, 1 tablespoon minced canned chipotle chili in adobo sauce, and ½ teaspoon salt; substitute this mixture for barbecue sauce mixture in step 1. Stir 1 tablespoon bourbon into sauce after thickening in step 3.

MAKING WINGS IN THE PRESSURE COOKER

Wings have two joints and three sections: the drumette, the flat midsection, and the wingtip. Sometimes you can buy wings broken down, but you might have to do it yourself. Use a chef's knife to cut through the joints. Discard the wingtips; they have no meat and will make the sauce greasy.

Cooking the wings in the pressure cooker right in the sauce means the wings and the sauce both get a flavor boost. Some of the fat in the skin also renders during cooking, which helps that skin crisp up nicely in the next step.

Once the wings are cooked through, we run them under the broiler. We do the broiling in two stages. The first 10-minute stage renders more fat and crisps up the skin. Be sure to flip them over halfway through this broiling time.

For the second 10- to 15-minute broiling stage, we brush the wings with sauce twice. This helps thicken the sauce and give the wings the classic sticky glazed coating. Again, be sure to flip the wings over and glaze both sides.

TROUBLESHOOTING

Can I just leave the wings whole?	Yes, you can leave them whole and skip the prep, but they will be much harder to maneuver under the broiler and more difficult to eat. The cooking time will remain the same.
Do I need to alter the recipe for a 6-quart electric pressure cooker?	Yes, quick release the pressure immediately after the pressurized cooking time; do not let the cooker switch to the warm setting. Increase the simmering time to 20 minutes in step 3, and use the browning (not the simmer) setting. Start broiling the wings halfway through the simmering time.

SIDES

Parmesan Risotto

WHY THIS RECIPE WORKS

A dish that typically requires near-constant stirring, risotto is probably low on most lists of weeknight side dish options. But not for home cooks with a pressure cooker. After sautéing aromatics and toasting the rice for a few minutes, we stirred in wine, then broth. Then, instead of stirring for up to 30 minutes, we simply locked on the lid and let the magic happen. Six minutes under pressure delivered risotto that was almost done. From that point, we simmered the risotto, stirring for just 6 minutes, until it was perfectly creamy. A little Parmesan was the only finishing touch needed for this simple recipe, although you may also garnish with parsley and shaved Parmesan, if desired.

INGREDIENTS

2	tablespoons unsalted butter
1	small onion, chopped fine
3	garlic cloves, minced
1½	cups Arborio rice
½	cup white wine
4	cups low-sodium chicken broth, warmed
1	ounce Parmesan cheese, grated (½ cup), plus extra for serving
	Salt and pepper

1. BUILD FLAVOR: Melt butter in pressure-cooker pot over medium-high heat. Add onion and cook until softened,

SERVES	TOTAL TIME
4	**ABOUT 30 MINUTES**

PRESSURE LEVEL	RELEASE
HIGH	**QUICK**

6 MINUTES
UNDER PRESSURE

about 5 minutes. Stir in garlic and cook until fragrant, about 30 seconds. Stir in rice and toast lightly, about 3 minutes. Stir in wine and cook until almost evaporated, about 1 minute. Stir in 3¼ cups broth. Using wooden spoon, scrape up any rice sticking to bottom of pot.

2. HIGH PRESSURE FOR 6 MINUTES: Lock pressure-cooker lid in place and bring to high pressure over medium-high heat. As soon as pot reaches high pressure, reduce heat to medium-low and cook for 6 minutes, adjusting heat as needed to maintain high pressure.

3. QUICK RELEASE PRESSURE: Remove pot from heat. Quick release pressure, then carefully remove lid, allowing steam to escape away from you.

4. BEFORE SERVING: Continue to cook risotto over medium heat, stirring constantly, until rice is tender and liquid has thickened, about 6 minutes. Stir in Parmesan and season with salt and pepper to taste. Before serving, add remaining ¾ cup broth as needed to loosen risotto consistency.

VARIATIONS

Butternut Squash and Sage Risotto
Add 8 ounces butternut squash, peeled and cut into ½-inch cubes (1⅓ cups), to pot with onion and cook until onion and squash are browned, about 10 minutes. Add 3 tablespoons chopped fresh sage to pot with garlic in step 1.

MAKING RISOTTO IN A PRESSURE COOKER

Pressure-cooker risotto starts just like traditional risotto. After sautéing our aromatics, we toast the rice for a few minutes in the pot. This deepens the rice's flavor and improves the final texture of the risotto by keeping it from turning overly starchy.

After cooking under pressure for just 6 minutes, the rice is well on its way to risotto. We slightly undercook it under pressure to account for slight variations among pressure cookers and rice grains, then finish it with another few minutes of stirring with the pot uncovered.

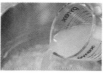

Once finished, the risotto will continue to thicken as it sits. Be ready to thin it out with additional broth before serving to loosen its consistency as necessary.

TROUBLESHOOTING

What if my risotto is too loose or seems gluey?	If it's loose, continue to simmer the risotto in step 4, stirring constantly and being careful not to scorch the pot, until it reaches the desired consistency. If it's gluey, add additional broth as needed. Note that as the risotto sits, it will thicken up naturally.
Do I need to alter the recipe for a 6-quart electric pressure cooker?	Yes, instead of relying on the cooker's built-in timer to keep track of the pressurized cooking time, use your own timer and start the countdown as soon as the pot comes to pressure. After the 6-minute cooking time, quick release the pressure immediately; do not let the cooker switch to the warm setting. Use the browning (not the simmer) setting to finish cooking the risotto in step 4.

Mushroom Risotto
Add 8 ounces cremini mushrooms, trimmed and sliced thin, to pot with onion and cook until onion and mushrooms are browned, about 10 minutes. Stir in ½ ounce dried porcini mushrooms, rinsed and minced, with garlic in step 1.

Creamy Polenta

SERVES	TOTAL TIME
6	**ABOUT 25 MINUTES**

PRESSURE LEVEL	RELEASE
HIGH	**QUICK**

10 MINUTES
UNDER PRESSURE

✔ WHY THIS RECIPE WORKS

When it comes to cooking polenta, the devil is in the details: Depending on the cornmeal's texture, it can take up to an hour to cook, and if you don't stir it almost constantly, polenta forms intractable lumps. The alternative, instant polenta, tends to serve up as a gluey, unappealing mass. Enter the pressure cooker. We started by combining our coarse-ground, traditionally slow-cooking polenta with plenty of water, then locked on the lid. After just 10 minutes of pressurized cooking time followed by a quick release, our polenta needed just 1 minute of thorough stirring to work out any small lumps and ensure there wouldn't be any scorching on the pot's bottom. Parmesan and butter stirred in just before serving gave our polenta the right salty, nutty finish.

INGREDIENTS

- **6** cups water
- **1½** cups coarse-ground polenta
  Salt and pepper
- **1½** ounces Parmesan cheese, grated (¾ cup), plus extra for serving
- **3** tablespoons unsalted butter, cut into chunks

1. HIGH PRESSURE FOR 10 MINUTES: Combine water, polenta, and 1 teaspoon salt in pressure-cooker pot. Lock pressure-cooker lid in place and bring to high pressure over medium-high heat. As soon as pot reaches high pressure, reduce heat to medium-low and cook for 10 minutes, adjusting heat as needed to maintain high pressure.

2. QUICK RELEASE PRESSURE: Remove pot from heat. Quick release pressure, then carefully remove lid, allowing steam to escape away from you.

3. BEFORE SERVING: Stir in Parmesan and butter. Using wooden spoon, scrape up any polenta that has stuck to bottom of pot then continue to stir until polenta is thick and creamy, about 1 minute. Season with salt and pepper to taste. Serve with extra Parmesan.

VARIATIONS

Sun-Dried Tomato and Basil Polenta

Add ⅓ cup oil-packed sun-dried tomatoes, rinsed and chopped, to pot with polenta in step 1. Stir ¼ cup chopped fresh basil into cooked polenta with Parmesan and butter.

Mushroom–Blue Cheese Polenta

Omit Parmesan. Add ½ ounce porcini mushrooms, rinsed and minced, and 1 sprig fresh thyme to pot with polenta in step 1. Sprinkle ¼ cup crumbled blue cheese over polenta and remove thyme sprig before serving.

MAKING POLENTA IN A PRESSURE COOKER

Making polenta in the pressure cooker couldn't be easier. Start by simply combining water, cornmeal, and a little salt in the pressure-cooker pot, then lock on the lid.

After 10 minutes of pressurized cooking time, it's important to quick release the pressure and open the lid quickly because if it cooks much longer, it will turn gluey and scorch on the bottom of the pot. Make sure to open the lid away from you so steam can escape safely.

As soon as the lid is off and the cloud of steam is gone, add the butter and Parmesan. These two simple additions will give the polenta some richness.

After adding the cheese and butter to the pot, immediately begin stirring the polenta with a wooden spoon, scraping at the bottom of the pot to incorporate any grains that might be stuck. Then continue to stir the polenta vigorously for a minute, until the polenta looks creamy.

TROUBLESHOOTING

Can I use products that are labeled cornmeal instead of polenta?

Products labeled "polenta" are in fact cornmeal; it's fine to use a product labeled "coarse-ground cornmeal." Just make sure it is evenly ground and has uniformly large grains. Be aware that grind size can vary greatly from brand to brand, so one manufacturer's coarse could be another's fine. Look for grains about the size of couscous. Also take a look at the package labeling. We love the full-corn flavor of whole-grain cornmeal, but it remains slightly gritty no matter how long you cook it. We prefer degerminated cornmeal, in which the hard hull and germ are removed from each kernel (if it's not explicitly labeled degerminated, you can assume it's whole-grain).

Do I need to alter the recipe for a 6-quart electric pressure cooker?

Yes, quick release the pressure immediately after the pressurized cooking time; do not let the cooker switch to the warm setting. Use the browning (not the simmer) setting to finish cooking the polenta in step 3.

Artichokes with Lemon-Garlic Butter

WHY THIS RECIPE WORKS

Whole artichokes with drawn butter make for a gorgeous first course, but the nearly 45-minute cooking time plus prep can make them a real turn-off, even for a special occasion. We suspected the pressure cooker could make a big difference here. After some quick prep, we placed four whole artichokes and 1 cup of water in our pressure-cooker pot and locked on the lid. Our artichokes were cooked through perfectly after just 15 minutes. While the artichokes cooked, we made a simple butter sauce for dipping the leaves. We melted butter in the microwave in a few seconds, adding some garlic for savory depth and lemon zest and juice for brightness and to cut the butter's richness. This recipe was so easy we knew we wouldn't be reserving artichokes just for special occasions anymore.

INGREDIENTS

- 4 whole artichokes (10 ounces each)
- 1 cup water
- 8 tablespoons unsalted butter, melted
- ¼ teaspoon grated lemon zest plus 1 tablespoon juice
- 1 garlic clove, minced
- ¼ teaspoon salt

SERVES	TOTAL TIME
4	ABOUT 30 MINUTES

PRESSURE LEVEL	RELEASE
HIGH	QUICK

15 MINUTES
UNDER PRESSURE

1. Using chef's knife, cut off stem so artichoke sits upright, then trim off top quarter of artichoke. Using kitchen shears, trim off top portion of outer leaves. Place artichokes, right side up, in pressure-cooker pot and add water.

2. HIGH PRESSURE FOR 15 MINUTES: Lock pressure-cooker lid in place and bring to high pressure over medium-high heat. As soon as pot reaches high pressure, reduce heat to medium-low and cook for 15 minutes, adjusting heat as needed to maintain high pressure.

3. QUICK RELEASE PRESSURE: Remove pot from heat. Quick release pressure, then carefully remove lid, allowing steam to escape away from you.

4. BEFORE SERVING: Microwave butter, lemon zest and juice, garlic, and salt together in bowl until melted, about 90 seconds. Whisk butter mixture to combine, then divide evenly between 4 serving bowls. Remove artichokes from pot, letting any excess water drain back into pot, place artichokes in bowls with butter, and serve.

MAKING ARTICHOKES IN A PRESSURE COOKER

To ensure even cooking, we found it best to sit the artichokes upright in the pressure cooker. To do this, you need to cut the stem off of each artichoke so that the base is even.

Cutting off the top quarter of the artichoke allows the heat to penetrate to the center of the artichoke more quickly and thus further ensures even cooking. The leaves at the top of the artichoke don't really have much meat to them anyway, so it's not a big loss.

The tip ends of an artichoke's leaves can be sharp, and we quickly learned they don't soften much during cooking. To avoid getting pricked when taking the artichokes out of the pressure cooker, we cut off the dry sharp tips of the outer leaves prior to cooking.

TROUBLESHOOTING

How do I know if the artichokes are done?	To test the artichokes for doneness, try pulling on a leaf. The leaf should slip out easily. If it doesn't, continue to simmer the artichokes gently, covered but not under pressure, until they are tender.
Can I substitute baby artichokes?	Yes, you can fit up to 8 baby artichokes in the pot at the same time. Reduce the pressurized cooking time to 5 minutes.
Can I cook just two artichokes this way?	Yes, and the pressurized cooking time will remain the same. Be sure to keep the artichokes upright during cooking; if necessary, prop them upright using balls of aluminum foil.
Can I double this recipe?	No, you can't fit more than 4 (10-ounce) artichokes upright in the pressure cooker pot at the same time. However, you can fit 6 (6-ounce) artichokes; the cooking time would remain the same.
Do I need to alter the recipe for a 6-quart electric pressure cooker?	Yes, quick release the pressure immediately after the pressurized cooking time; do not let the cooker switch to the warm setting.

Braised Beets with Dill Vinaigrette

WHY THIS RECIPE WORKS

Roasting and steaming beets can take up to an hour, but the pressure cooker delivers tender beets with undiluted earthy-sweet flavor and bright color in one-third the time. For even cooking, we halved smaller beets and quartered the larger ones. Paper towels helped us quickly skin the cooked beets, then we cut them into wedges. Tossing them with a simple dressing that we brightened with lemon juice, red wine vinegar, and fresh dill gave us a side dish that we could pair with almost any meal.

INGREDIENTS

- 6 (3- to 5-ounce) beets, trimmed
- 1 cup water
- 3 tablespoons extra-virgin olive oil
- 1 small shallot, minced
- 1 tablespoon minced fresh dill
- 1 tablespoon lemon juice
- 1 teaspoon red wine vinegar
- Salt and pepper

1. Halve beets weighing 3 to 4 ounces and quarter beets weighing 4 to 5 ounces. Add beets and water to pressure-cooker pot.

2. HIGH PRESSURE FOR 20 MINUTES: Lock pressure-cooker lid in place and bring to high pressure over medium-high heat. As soon as pot reaches high pressure, reduce heat to medium-low and cook for 20 minutes, adjusting heat as needed to maintain high pressure.

SERVES	TOTAL TIME
4	ABOUT 30 MINUTES

PRESSURE LEVEL	RELEASE
HIGH	QUICK

20 MINUTES

UNDER PRESSURE

3. QUICK RELEASE PRESSURE: Remove pot from heat. Quick release pressure, then carefully remove lid, allowing steam to escape away from you.

4. BEFORE SERVING: Transfer beets to plate, let cool slightly, then rub off skins using paper towels. Slice beets into ½-inch-thick wedges.

5. Whisk oil, shallot, dill, lemon juice, and vinegar together in medium bowl, add warm beets, and toss to coat. Season with salt and pepper to taste, and serve.

VARIATIONS

Braised Beets with Sesame-Ginger Vinaigrette
Substitute following mixture for dill vinaigrette in step 5: 2 tablespoons rice vinegar, 1 tablespoon toasted sesame oil, 1 tablespoon olive oil, 2 thinly sliced scallions, 2 teaspoons grated fresh ginger, ½ teaspoon grated orange zest, and 1 tablespoon orange juice.

Beet, Apple, and Walnut Salad
Substitute following mixture for dill vinaigrette in step 5: 3 tablespoons extra-virgin olive oil, 1½ tablespoons white wine vinegar, and 1 tablespoon minced fresh parsley. Add 1 Granny Smith apple, cored and sliced thin, and ½ cup walnuts, toasted and coarsely chopped, to vinaigrette with cooked beets. Sprinkle with ½ cup crumbled blue cheese before serving.

MAKING BRAISED BEETS IN A PRESSURE COOKER

The pressure cooker cuts the cooking time of beets substantially, and we found cutting the beets into evenly sized pieces—large beets into quarters and smaller beets into halves—reduces the cooking time further and ensures even cooking.

Once the beets are cooked, the skins will come off easily. You could use your fingers to do this job, although we prefer rubbing the skins off with paper towels to cut down on the mess.

For salad-friendly beets, we cut the cooked and peeled beets into smaller ½-inch-thick wedges.

Tossing the beets in the vinaigrette while they are still slightly warm helps them absorb the flavors a little better.

TROUBLESHOOTING

How do I know if my beets are cooked properly?	You'll know the beets are cooked properly if a paring knife can easily be inserted into the center and there's little resistance. If they aren't done after releasing pressure, add 1 cup water to the pot and continue to simmer until done.
Will this recipe work with golden beets as well as red?	We used red beets during our testing but golden beets should also work fine. Golden beets taste a little less sweet and a little less earthy than red beets.
Do I need to alter the recipe for a 6-quart electric pressure cooker?	Yes, quick release the pressure immediately after the pressurized cooking time; do not let the cooker switch to the warm setting.

Braised Collard Greens with Bacon

WHY THIS RECIPE WORKS

To keep this Southern favorite simple, we first tried pressure cooking greens in a little broth, then simmering to reduce the liquid to a make a flavorful pot likker. But with so little liquid in the pot, we found the cooking was uneven, and the greens' bitterness was concentrated in the pot likker. We got better results by cooking our greens in ample water until they were just underdone, then draining and simmering them in some broth plus aromatics until tender. Crisping some chopped bacon in the pot before adding the greens left behind rendered fat that gave our greens meaty appeal, while a few teaspoons of vinegar added at the end lent a balancing brightness.

INGREDIENTS

- 2 **pounds collard greens, stemmed and chopped (see page 31)**
- 1 **quart water**
  Salt and pepper
- 2 **slices bacon, chopped fine**
- 1 **tablespoon vegetable oil**
- 1 **small onion, chopped fine**
- 2 **garlic cloves, minced**
- ⅛ **teaspoon red pepper flakes**
- 2 **cups low-sodium chicken broth**
- 2 **teaspoons cider vinegar**

1. HIGH PRESSURE FOR 10 MINUTES: Combine collard greens, water, and 1 teaspoon salt in pressure-cooker pot. Lock pressure-cooker lid in place and bring to high pressure over

SERVES	TOTAL TIME
4 TO 6	**ABOUT 45 MINUTES**

PRESSURE LEVEL	RELEASE
HIGH	**QUICK**

10 MINUTES

UNDER PRESSURE

medium-high heat. As soon as pot reaches high pressure, reduce heat to medium-low and cook for 10 minutes, adjusting heat as needed to maintain high pressure.

2. QUICK RELEASE PRESSURE: Remove pot from heat. Quick release pressure, then carefully remove lid, allowing steam to escape away from you.

3. BEFORE SERVING: Drain greens in colander. Add bacon and oil to now-empty pot and cook over medium heat until well browned, about 5 minutes; transfer to paper towel–lined plate.

4. Add onion and ¼ teaspoon salt to fat left in pot and cook over medium-high heat until softened, about 5 minutes. Stir in garlic and pepper flakes and cook until fragrant, about 30 seconds. Stir in drained greens. Add broth and simmer until greens are tender and sauce is flavorful, about 10 minutes. Off heat, stir in vinegar and season with salt and pepper to taste. Sprinkle with bacon and serve.

VARIATION

Braised Kale with Chorizo
Substitute 2 pounds kale, stemmed and chopped, for collard greens and reduce pressurized cooking time to 7 minutes. Substitute 2 ounces chorizo sausage, cut into ½-inch pieces, for bacon and cook in step 3 until lightly browned, about 3 minutes. Omit vinegar.

COOKING COLLARD GREENS IN A PRESSURE COOKER

For even cooking, we cook the greens under pressure with a full quart of water. The cooking water is too bitter to double as the pot likker (and there's too much of it anyway), so we drain the greens after 10 minutes of cooking.

To give our greens a hit of meaty pork flavor, we crisp a couple of chopped bacon slices in the empty pot. We set the crisped bits aside for garnishing the greens before serving.

After sautéing some onion in the rendered bacon fat, we add garlic and red pepper flakes, then stir in the greens and 2 cups of broth. Simmering the greens for 10 minutes makes them perfectly tender and infuses the liquid with flavor, giving us a tasty pot likker for pouring over our greens.

Just 2 teaspoons of cider vinegar adds the right amount of brightness to balance out this side dish.

TROUBLESHOOTING

Can I make this dish vegetarian?	Yes, omit the bacon and add 3 tablespoons olive oil to the pot with the onion in step 4. Also, substitute 2 cups vegetable broth for the chicken broth.
Can I double the recipe?	No, even though the greens wilt once cooked, fitting twice as many raw greens into the pot isn't possible.
Do I need to alter the recipe for a 6-quart stovetop or an electric pressure cooker?	Two pounds of collards will overfill a 6-quart pot, but you can make half the recipe; the pressurized cooking time will remain the same. If using an electric pressure cooker, quick release the pressure immediately after the pressurized cooking time; do not let the cooker switch to the warm setting. Also, increase the simmering time to 15 minutes in step 4, and use the browning (not the simmer) setting.

Braised Red Cabbage

✓ WHY THIS RECIPE WORKS

Braising humble cabbage transforms it by bringing out its sweet flavor and giving it a silky texture. Sweet-and-sour braised red cabbage is a classic German side that has a bright flavor ideal for pairing with rich, meaty entrées. Since braising it in a Dutch oven can take longer than a main course to cook, we used our pressure cooker to turn it into a quick, more convenient side. Sautéing bacon and onion in the pot first built up some flavorful fond that we could incorporate into the braising liquid. Juniper and allspice lent traditional warm-spice flavor and aroma (just make sure not to eat the juniper berries in the final dish). For the sweet component, brown sugar was a good start. Cider vinegar seemed like the right choice for the sour, but when we added it to the braising liquid (we opted for chicken broth) prior to cooking its flavor got washed out. Instead, we added 1 tablespoon of cider vinegar to the pot after the cabbage was cooked for a fresher hit of flavor. And a surprising ingredient, a Granny Smith apple, actually lent both sweet and tart flavors to the cabbage, and by chopping it into ¼-inch pieces and cooking it under pressure, the apple melted into the cabbage. After 10 minutes under pressure, we found the cabbage needed about 10 more minutes of simmering, uncovered, so that the braising liquid could reduce. Adding a little more sugar along with cider vinegar at the end brought the sweet-and-sour flavor to the fore.

SERVES	TOTAL TIME
4 TO 6	**ABOUT 45 MINUTES**

PRESSURE LEVEL	RELEASE
HIGH	**QUICK**

10 MINUTES
UNDER PRESSURE

INGREDIENTS

2	slices bacon, chopped fine
1	onion, chopped medium
5	juniper berries (optional)
¼	teaspoon ground allspice
1½	teaspoons minced fresh thyme or ½ teaspoon dried
2	bay leaves
1	head red cabbage (2 pounds), cored and sliced ¼ inch thick
1	Granny Smith apple, peeled, cored, and chopped
½	cup low-sodium chicken broth
1	tablespoon brown sugar, plus extra as needed
	Salt and pepper
1	tablespoon cider vinegar

1. BUILD FLAVOR: Cook bacon and onion in pressure-cooker pot over medium heat until bacon is crisp and onion is browned, about 10 minutes. Stir in juniper berries (if using), allspice, thyme, and bay leaves and cook until fragrant, about 30 seconds. Stir in cabbage, apple, broth, brown sugar, and 1 teaspoon salt.

2. HIGH PRESSURE FOR 10 MINUTES: Lock pressure-cooker lid in place and bring to high pressure over medium-high heat. As soon as pot reaches high pressure, reduce heat to medium-low and cook for 10 minutes, adjusting heat as needed to maintain high pressure.

TEST KITCHEN TIP CUTTING UP RED CABBAGE

1. Cut cabbage into quarters, then cut away hard piece of core attached to each quarter.

2. Separate cabbage into small stacks of leaves, then flatten on cutting board and use chef's knife to cut stack of leaves crosswise into ¼-inch-wide shreds.

TROUBLESHOOTING

Can another type of cabbage work in this recipe?	No, other types of cabbage, such as green cabbage, napa cabbage, and Chinese cabbage, cannot be substituted for the red cabbage in this recipe.
Can I use the preshredded cabbage sold at the market?	No, this cabbage is sliced too finely and disintegrates when cooked under pressure. We also found its flavor to be quite dry and sour.
Can I make this recipe vegetarian?	Yes. Omit the bacon, add 2 tablespoons olive oil to the pot with the onion in step 1, and substitute vegetable broth for the chicken broth.
Do I need to alter the recipe for a 6-quart electric pressure cooker?	Yes, quick release the pressure immediately after the pressurized cooking time; do not let the cooker switch to the warm setting. Increase the simmering time to 15 minutes in step 4, and use the browning (not the simmer) setting.

3. QUICK RELEASE PRESSURE: Remove pot from heat. Quick release pressure, then carefully remove lid, allowing steam to escape away from you.

4. BEFORE SERVING: Continue to cook cabbage over medium heat, stirring often, until most of the liquid has evaporated, about 10 minutes. Stir in vinegar and season with salt, pepper, and extra sugar to taste. Serve.

Mashed Butternut Squash

✓ **WHY THIS RECIPE WORKS**

Mashed butternut squash is a silky-smooth, earthy-sweet side dish that is elegant and down-home at once. To achieve the right texture, we typically steam chunks of squash for 30 minutes, then transfer them to the food processor to puree. To evenly cook 2½ pounds of butternut squash under pressure, we found we needed a full cup of water in the pot. The pressure cooker broke down the fibers of the squash so well that running it in the food processor was overkill—it turned our winter squash into whipped baby food. So instead, we returned the chunks of squash to the pot and simply mashed them with a potato masher. Half-and-half added just enough richness, along with butter and a few tablespoons of brown sugar for a complementary sweetness.

INGREDIENTS

2½	pounds butternut squash, peeled, seeded, and cut into 1-inch chunks (8 cups)
1	cup water
	Salt and pepper
¼	cup half-and-half
4	tablespoons unsalted butter
2	tablespoons packed brown sugar, plus extra as needed

1. HIGH PRESSURE FOR 12 MINUTES: Combine squash, water, and ½ teaspoon salt in pressure-cooker pot. Lock pressure-cooker lid in place and bring to high pressure over medium-high heat.

SERVES	TOTAL TIME
4 TO 6	**ABOUT 25 MINUTES**

PRESSURE LEVEL	RELEASE
HIGH	**QUICK**

12 MINUTES
UNDER PRESSURE

As soon as pot reaches high pressure, reduce heat to medium-low and cook for 12 minutes, adjusting heat as needed to maintain high pressure.

2. QUICK RELEASE PRESSURE: Remove pot from heat. Quick release pressure, then carefully remove lid, allowing steam to escape away from you.

3. BEFORE SERVING: Drain squash in colander and toss gently to remove excess water. Return drained squash to now-empty pot and mash with potato masher until mostly smooth. Fold in half-and-half, butter, and sugar. Season with salt, pepper, and extra sugar to taste. Serve.

VARIATIONS

Mashed Chipotle-Honey Butternut Squash

Omit sugar. Add 3 tablespoons honey and 1½–2 teaspoons minced canned chipotle chile in adobo sauce to pot with half-and-half and butter in step 3.

Mashed Warm-Spiced Butternut Squash

After draining cooked squash in step 3, set aside. Add butter, ½ teaspoon ground ginger, ½ teaspoon ground cinnamon, and ¼ teaspoon ground nutmeg to now-empty pot and cook over medium heat until fragrant, about 1 minute. Off heat, return drained squash to pot and continue with recipe as directed.

TEST KITCHEN TIP CUTTING UP BUTTERNUT SQUASH

When preparing butternut squash, we find it easiest to peel the squash and then divide it into two sections, the long neck and the curved bottom, before cutting it into chunks.

1. After cutting bottom section in half vertically, scoop out seeds and fibers with large spoon. Slice each half into evenly sized lengths, then cut lengths into chunks according to recipe.

2. Cut neck section into evenly sized planks, then cut planks into chunks according to recipe.

TROUBLESHOOTING

Can I use another type of squash in this recipe?	Yes, we had great results swapping in delicata, kabocha, and hubbard squash for the butternut squash in this recipe. We do not suggest using sugar pumpkins.
Can I double the recipe?	Yes, you can double the recipe; increase the pressurized cooking time to 17 minutes.
Do I need to alter the recipe for a 6-quart electric pressure cooker?	Yes, quick release the pressure immediately after the pressurized cooking time; do not let the cooker switch to the warm setting. Be sure to use a potato masher that won't scratch nonstick surfaces.

Mashed Maple-Orange Butternut Squash

Omit sugar. Add 2 tablespoons maple syrup and 1½ tablespoons orange marmalade to pot with half-and-half and butter in step 3.

Mashed Sweet Potatoes

SERVES **4**	TOTAL TIME **ABOUT 25 MINUTES**	**15** **MINUTES** UNDER PRESSURE
PRESSURE LEVEL **HIGH**	RELEASE **QUICK**	

✓ WHY THIS RECIPE WORKS

Mashed sweet potatoes are as much at home on the family dinner table alongside pork chops as they are on the celebratory Thanksgiving spread. We wanted a simple, slightly rich side with deep, earthy sweetness. For even cooking, we cut the potatoes into even slices and cooked them under pressure along with a cup of water. In just 15 minutes, the pressure cooker had done a great job of turning the potatoes ultratender while maintaining their bright orange color and concentrating their earthy flavor. After draining the potatoes and returning them to the pot, some quick work with a masher turned them into the side we were after. All they needed was some butter, cream, and sugar, and they were ready for the table.

INGREDIENTS

- 2 **pounds sweet potatoes, peeled and sliced ½ inch thick**
- 1 **cup water**
  Salt and pepper
- 4 **tablespoons unsalted butter, cut into 4 pieces**
- 2 **tablespoons heavy cream**
- 1 **teaspoon sugar**

1. HIGH PRESSURE FOR 15 MINUTES: Combine sweet potatoes, water, and ½ teaspoon salt in pressure-cooker pot. Lock pressure-cooker lid in place and bring to high pressure over medium-high heat. As soon as pot reaches high pressure, reduce heat to medium-low and cook for 15 minutes, adjusting heat as needed to maintain high pressure.

2. QUICK RELEASE PRESSURE: Remove pot from heat. Quick release pressure, then carefully remove lid, allowing steam to escape away from you.

3. BEFORE SERVING: Drain sweet potatoes in colander and toss gently to remove excess water. Return drained sweet potatoes to now-empty pot and mash with potato masher until mostly smooth. Fold in butter, cream, and sugar. Season with salt and pepper to taste, and serve.

VARIATIONS

Mashed Sweet Potatoes with Indian Spices

After draining potatoes in step 3, melt butter in now-empty pot, add ¾ teaspoon garam masala, and cook over medium heat until fragrant, about 30 seconds. Off heat, return drained potatoes to pot and mash as directed. Add ½ cup currants to pot with heavy cream and sugar.

Mashed Sweet Potatoes with Cinnamon and Sugar

Increase amount of sugar to 3 tablespoons. After draining potatoes in step 3, add butter and 1 teaspoon cinnamon to now-empty pot and cook over medium heat until fragrant, about 1 minute. Off heat, return drained potatoes to pot and continue with recipe as directed.

MAKING MASHED SWEET POTATOES IN A PRESSURE COOKER

Sweet potatoes are typically unevenly shaped and odd sizes, so cutting them crosswise into slices of even thickness helps ensure even cooking without requiring a whole lot of knife work.

We cook the potatoes under pressure with a full cup of water. This also ensures even cooking and prevents scorching, but you can't leave that water in the pot or you'll end up with a watery, loose side dish. Once the potatoes are cooked, drain them in a colander.

The pressure cooker does a great job of turning the potatoes tender in just 15 minutes. There's no need to break out the food processor for this step; a potato masher does a great job of mashing them to the right consistency without requiring a lot of effort.

Butter, cream, and sugar are all the additions this classic side dish needs before it's ready for the table.

TROUBLESHOOTING

Can I double this recipe?	Yes, you can double the recipe; increase the pressurized cooking time to 20 minutes.
Can I substitute yams for the sweet potatoes?	Yes. Yams range in color from white to light yellow to pink, so obviously you won't end up with the classic orange-colored side dish, but the recipe will still work fine. Just substitute an equal amount of yams and prep and cook them as directed for the sweet potatoes.
Can I substitute milk for the cream?	Yes, either milk or half-and-half can be substituted for the cream. We don't recommend using skim milk, however, which will result in thin, watery potatoes.
Do I need to alter the recipe for a 6-quart electric pressure cooker?	Yes, quick release the pressure immediately after the pressurized cooking time; do not let the cooker switch to the warm setting. Be sure to use a potato masher that won't scratch nonstick surfaces.

Mashed Potatoes

✔ **WHY THIS RECIPE WORKS**
It's all too common for mashed potatoes to turn out pasty, gluey, or dry. We wanted ultrasmooth, creamy, yet light and fluffy mashed potatoes with a hint of richness. Plus, we didn't want to spend a lot of time or effort putting this simple side together. It took no time to bring the pressure-cooker pot with 2 pounds of russets and 1 cup of water up to high pressure, and after 8 minutes of cooking we quick released the pressure and drained the potatoes. Because russets are starchy, we found it important, even after draining the potatoes in a colander, to quickly cook off any excess water on the potatoes prior to mashing them or else they turned out gluey. Depending on the age of the potatoes, we found the amount of half-and-half necessary varied, so we folded in ⅔ cup after adding the butter, then seasoned the potatoes, and added more dairy as needed just before serving to loosen them up.

INGREDIENTS

2 pounds russet potatoes, peeled and sliced ½ inch thick

1 cup water
   Salt and pepper

8 tablespoons unsalted butter, melted

1 cup half-and-half, hot

SERVES	TOTAL TIME	
4 TO 6	**ABOUT 25 MINUTES**	**8**
PRESSURE LEVEL	RELEASE	**MINUTES**
HIGH	**QUICK**	**UNDER PRESSURE**

1. HIGH PRESSURE FOR 8 MINUTES: Place potatoes, water, and ½ teaspoon salt in pressure-cooker pot. Lock pressure-cooker lid in place and bring to high pressure over medium-high heat. As soon as pot reaches high pressure, reduce heat to medium-low and cook for 8 minutes, adjusting heat as needed to maintain high pressure.

2. QUICK RELEASE PRESSURE: Remove pot from heat. Quick release pressure, then carefully remove lid, allowing steam to escape away from you.

3. BEFORE SERVING: Drain potatoes in colander and toss gently to remove excess water. Return drained potatoes to now-empty pot and cook over medium heat, stirring often, until all excess water has evaporated, about 1 minute. Off heat, mash with potato masher until smooth. Gently fold in melted butter. Gently fold in ⅔ cup half-and-half and season with salt and pepper to taste. Before serving, fold in remaining ⅓ cup half-and-half as needed to adjust consistency.

VARIATIONS

Pesto Mashed Potatoes
Substitute ½ cup pesto for butter.

Garlicky Mashed Potatoes
Add 10 peeled garlic cloves to pot with potatoes in step 1. Mash cooked garlic with potatoes in step 3.

MAKING MASHED POTATOES IN A PRESSURE COOKER

Russets make the best mashed potatoes because they are high in starch and low in water content, which translates to a fluffy, full texture and a nice ability to absorb dairy without becoming gummy. Be sure to cut the peeled potatoes into uniformly sized slices so that they cook at the same rate.

You need 1 cup of water in the pot with the potatoes to ensure even cooking. Once the potatoes are done, drain them in a colander, then return them to the pot.

We found when mashing russet potatoes, there is more potential than with other vegetables for starchy, gluey results. We discovered that after draining the potatoes, it was key to return them to the pot and heat them for a minute to drive off any excess moisture before proceeding.

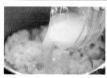
It's important to add the butter to the pot before the cream. If the cream goes in first, its water content works with the starch in the potatoes and turns the texture gluey. Adding the butter first coats the starch in fat and leads to silky, creamy, smooth mashed potatoes.

TROUBLESHOOTING

Can I substitute Yukon Gold or generic white potatoes here?
Yes, however the final flavor and texture will be different. Medium-starch Yukon Gold potatoes have a mild, buttery flavor and creamy texture, while white potatoes taste a bit more bland.

Can I double the recipe?
Yes, you can double the recipe; increase the pressurized cooking time to 12 minutes.

Do I need to alter the recipe for a 6-quart electric pressure cooker?
Yes, instead of relying on the cooker's built-in timer to keep track of the pressurized cooking time, use your own timer and start the countdown as soon as the pot comes to pressure. After the 8-minute cooking time, quick release the pressure immediately; do not let the cooker switch to the warm setting. Be sure to use a potato masher that won't scratch nonstick surfaces.

Buttermilk Smashed Red Potatoes

✓ **WHY THIS RECIPE WORKS**

For a country-style potato side dish, we started with red potatoes. Leaving the peels on kept the prep simple and helped lend the right rustic feel to the final dish. We also found we could put potatoes ranging from 2 to 3 inches in diameter whole into the pressure cooker; potatoes larger than that we simply halved. After 12 minutes under pressure, we drained the potatoes, returned them to the pot, and mashed them. We made sure to leave a few larger chunks intact. With its hint of sourness, a cup of buttermilk took the dish in the right direction, while sour cream ramped up the richness without making the texture pasty. Chopped chives added good color and a touch of freshness.

INGREDIENTS

- 2 **pounds medium red potatoes, scrubbed**
- 4 **cups water**
  Salt and pepper
- 1 **cup buttermilk, hot**
- ¼ **cup sour cream**
- 2 **tablespoons unsalted butter, cut into ¼-inch pieces**
- 3 **tablespoons minced fresh chives**

1. HIGH PRESSURE FOR 13 MINUTES: Place potatoes, water, and ½ teaspoon salt in pressure-cooker pot. Lock pressure-cooker lid in place and bring to high pressure over medium-high heat. As soon as pot reaches high pressure,

SERVES	TOTAL TIME	**13**
4 TO 6	**ABOUT 30 MINUTES**	**MINUTES**
PRESSURE LEVEL	RELEASE	
HIGH	**QUICK**	**UNDER PRESSURE**

reduce heat to medium-low and cook for 13 minutes, adjusting heat as needed to maintain high pressure.

2. QUICK RELEASE PRESSURE: Remove pot from heat. Quick release pressure, then carefully remove lid, allowing steam to escape away from you.

3. BEFORE SERVING: Drain potatoes in colander and toss gently to remove excess water. Return drained potatoes to now-empty pot and mash coarsely with potato masher, leaving some larger chunks. Fold in ½ cup buttermilk, sour cream, butter, chives, ½ teaspoon salt, and ⅛ teaspoon pepper. Before serving, fold in remaining ½ cup buttermilk as needed to adjust consistency.

VARIATIONS

Smashed Red Potatoes with Garlic and Scallions
Add 5 peeled garlic cloves to pot with potatoes in step 1. Substitute 6 thinly sliced scallions and ¼ cup minced parsley for chives.

Smashed Red Potatoes with Blue Cheese and Bacon
After draining potatoes in step 3, cook 3 slices finely chopped bacon in now-empty pot over medium-high heat until crisp, about 5 minutes; transfer to paper towel–lined plate. Off heat, return drained potatoes to pot, mash, and fold in remaining ingredients along with crisp bacon and ¼ cup crumbled blue cheese.

MAKING SMASHED RED POTATOES IN A PRESSURE COOKER

Since the skins are going to be in the final dish, it's important to scrub them well to ensure there is no dirt or grit left behind.

Since these potatoes are just 2 to 3 inches in diameter, there's no need to cut them before cooking. Even left whole, they only need 13 minutes under pressure to cook through. If you have any larger potatoes, simply cut those in half.

Once the potatoes are cooked and drained, return them to the pot and mash to a coarse consistency with a potato masher. Don't be tempted to try and mash these potatoes smooth. That will cause the skins to clump together.

For potatoes with the right consistency and good tangy flavor, we add both buttermilk and sour cream along with the butter and chives. The potatoes can stiffen up or look dry by serving time if they sit for a bit, but stirring in a little more buttermilk will get them back to the right consistency.

TROUBLESHOOTING

Is there a substitute for the buttermilk?	Yes, you can substitute ¾ cup plain whole-milk or low-fat yogurt thinned with ¼ cup milk for the buttermilk.
What if my potatoes are either very small or very large?	Using uniformly sized potatoes is most important for this recipe, so that they will cook through evenly and at the same rate. If using small potatoes (1 to 2 inches in diameter), reduce the pressurized cooking time to 12 minutes. If using large potatoes (larger than 3 inches), cut them in half prior to cooking. If the potatoes seem underdone after releasing the pressure, continue to simmer them on the stove top as needed until tender.
Do I need to alter the recipe for a 6-quart electric pressure cooker?	Yes, quick release the pressure immediately after the pressurized cooking time; do not let the cooker switch to the warm setting. Be sure to use a potato masher that won't scratch nonstick surfaces.

Warm Potato Salad

SERVES	TOTAL TIME
4 TO 6	**ABOUT 30 MINUTES**

PRESSURE LEVEL	RELEASE
HIGH	**QUICK**

7 MINUTES
UNDER PRESSURE

✓ WHY THIS RECIPE WORKS

You don't often think of salad and pressure cooker in the same sentence, but we realized using our pressure cooker was perfect for making a quick batch of warm German-style potato salad. Adding vinegar to the cooking water helped our potato chunks retain their shape during the brief 7-minute cooking time. We built up the dressing by cooking bacon in the pot, then some red onion in the rendered fat. After adding vinegar and some of the potato cooking water, we simmered it down to ensure concentrated flavor. Whole-grain mustard added the right bite, then we tossed in the potatoes, bacon, and some parsley, and our salad was ready. You can serve this salad cold too; simply season to taste before serving.

INGREDIENTS

- 2 **pounds red potatoes, cut into ¾-inch pieces**
- 1½ **cups water**
- 6 **tablespoons distilled white vinegar**
  Salt and pepper
- 4 **slices bacon, chopped fine**
- 1 **small red onion, chopped fine**
- 1¼ **teaspoons sugar**
- 2 **teaspoons whole-grain mustard**
- 3 **tablespoons minced fresh parsley**

1. HIGH PRESSURE FOR 7 MINUTES: Place potatoes, water, 2 tablespoons vinegar, and ½ teaspoon salt in pressure-cooker pot. Lock pressure-cooker lid in place and bring to high pressure over medium-high heat. As soon as pot reaches high pressure, reduce heat to medium-low and cook for 7 minutes, adjusting heat as needed to maintain high pressure.

2. QUICK RELEASE PRESSURE: Remove pot from heat. Quick release pressure, then carefully remove lid, allowing steam to escape away from you.

3. BEFORE SERVING: Reserve ¾ cup potato cooking water, then drain potatoes in colander and toss gently to remove excess water. Cook bacon in now-empty pot over medium-high heat until crisp, about 5 minutes; transfer to paper towel–lined plate. Pour off all but 4 tablespoons bacon fat.

4. Add onion and sugar to fat left in pot and cook over medium heat until softened and beginning to brown, about 4 minutes. Stir in remaining ¼ cup vinegar and ½ cup reserved cooking water and simmer until dressing measures ⅔ cup, about 3 minutes. Off heat, whisk in mustard. Add drained potatoes, bacon, and parsley and toss to coat. Season with salt and pepper to taste. Before serving, fold in remaining cooking water as needed to adjust consistency.

VARIATIONS

Warm French Potato Salad
Omit bacon and sugar. Substitute 6 tablespoons white wine vinegar for distilled white vinegar, 2 teaspoons Dijon mustard for whole-grain mustard,

MAKING POTATO SALAD IN A PRESSURE COOKER

Cutting the potatoes into ¾-inch pieces means that they will cook through quickly, and their uniform size ensures they cook through at the same rate.

We found that adding just 2 tablespoons of vinegar to the cooking water helps prevent the potatoes from breaking down and busting apart during cooking.

Once the potatoes are cooked, don't forget to reserve some of the cooking water before draining the potatoes. That cooking water lends flavor to the dressing and helps give it the right consistency.

We build the warm bacon-and-vinegar dressing right in the pot, then fold in the warm potatoes. Be gentle when folding the potatoes to keep them from falling apart.

TROUBLESHOOTING

Do I need to alter the recipe for a 6-quart electric pressure cooker?

Yes, instead of relying on the cooker's built-in timer to keep track of the pressurized cooking time, use your own timer and start the countdown as soon as the pot comes to pressure. After the 7-minute cooking time, quick release the pressure immediately; do not let the cooker switch to the warm setting. Use the browning (not the simmer) setting to simmer the dressing in steps 3 and 4.

and 2 tablespoons minced fresh tarragon for parsley. Add ¼ cup extra-virgin olive oil to pot with onion in step 4.

Warm Lemon-Dill Potato Salad
Omit bacon and sugar. Substitute 2 tablespoons white wine vinegar for

distilled white vinegar, 1 teaspoon Dijon mustard for whole-grain mustard, and 3 tablespoons minced fresh dill for parsley. Add ¼ cup extra-virgin olive oil to pot with onion in step 4. Add 3 tablespoons lemon juice with reserved cooking water in step 4.

Barbecued Beans

WHY THIS RECIPE WORKS

The 4 hours barbecued beans traditionally require is a long stint just for a side. Cooking the beans in the sauce was a no-go. The acidic sauce slowed the cooking, and the small amount of sauce in the pot wasn't enough to cook the beans evenly. So we cooked our beans under pressure in water (plus oil to prevent foaming) until they were done. After building the sauce, we returned the beans to the pot to finish with the sauce. Use small white beans (labeled as such) or navy beans in this recipe.

INGREDIENTS

- 1 **pound dried small white beans or navy beans (2 cups), picked over, rinsed, and salt-soaked (see page 18)**
- 2 **tablespoons vegetable oil**
- 4 **quarts plus 2 cups water**
  Salt and pepper
- 1 **onion, chopped fine**
- 2 **garlic cloves, minced**
- 2 **teaspoons chili powder**
- 1 **cup ketchup**
- ½ **cup molasses**
- 3 **tablespoons cider vinegar**
- 3 **tablespoons Dijon mustard**
- 1 **tablespoon brown sugar**

1. HIGH PRESSURE FOR 8 MINUTES: Combine beans and 1 tablespoon oil in pressure-cooker pot and stir to combine. Add 4 quarts water and 1 teaspoon salt. Lock pressure-cooker lid in place and bring to high pressure over

SERVES	TOTAL TIME
4 TO 6	**ABOUT 1¼ HOURS***

PRESSURE LEVEL	RELEASE
HIGH	**NATURAL**

*PLUS BEAN SOAKING TIME

8
MINUTES
UNDER PRESSURE

medium-high heat. As soon as pot reaches high pressure, reduce heat to medium-low and cook for 8 minutes, adjusting heat as needed to maintain high pressure.

2. NATURALLY RELEASE PRESSURE: Remove pot from heat and allow pressure to release naturally for 15 minutes. Quick release any remaining pressure, then carefully remove lid, allowing steam to escape away from you.

3. BUILD SAUCE: Taste beans for doneness; simmer beans gently as needed until tender. Drain cooked beans in colander. Heat remaining 1 tablespoon oil in now-empty pot over medium heat until shimmering. Add onion and cook until softened, about 5 minutes. Stir in garlic and chili powder and cook until fragrant, about 30 seconds. Stir in remaining 2 cups water, ketchup, molasses, vinegar, mustard, sugar, ½ teaspoon salt, and 1 teaspoon pepper, scraping up any browned bits.

4. BEFORE SERVING: Stir in drained beans and simmer until sauce has thickened, 10 to 15 minutes. Season with salt and pepper to taste and serve.

VARIATION

Boston "Baked" Beans

Omit chili powder and ketchup. Reduce amount of cider vinegar to 2 teaspoons. Add 4 ounces salt pork, trimmed of rind and cut into 1-inch pieces, to pot with onion in step 3 and cook until lightly browned, about 7 minutes.

MAKING BARBECUED BEANS IN A PRESSURE COOKER

 Soaking the beans is critical to ensure that the beans cook through evenly and that they hold together. It requires some thinking ahead, but all you have to do is combine the beans with water and a little salt and let them sit overnight.

 We tried cooking the beans directly in the sauce, but the sauce was so acidic it slowed down the beans' cooking, and the beans needed more liquid to cook evenly. So we use water to cook the beans most of the way through under pressure, then drain and finish them in the sauce.

 Once the drained beans are set aside, we build up the sauce, and letting the beans finish cooking in the sauce allows them to take on a lot of flavor. The simmering time also allows the sauce to thicken to the right consistency.

TROUBLESHOOTING

Can I double this recipe?	No. In order to cook 2 pounds of beans you'd need at least 8 quarts of water, which would overfill the pot.
Will this recipe fit in a 6-quart pot?	No, it would overfill the pot, but a half-recipe will work. Reduce all ingredients by half, except for the vinegar and mustard, which should both be reduced to 1 tablespoon. Reduce the pressurized cooking time to 6 minutes. If the beans taste underdone after releasing the pressure, simmer them gently until completely tender before building the sauce in step 3.
Do I need to alter the recipe for a 6-quart electric pressure cooker?	Yes, follow the 6-quart pot instructions above. And instead of relying on the cooker's built-in timer to keep track of the pressurized cooking time, use your own timer and start the countdown as soon as the pot comes to pressure. After the 6-minute cooking time, turn the cooker off immediately and let the pressure release naturally for 15 minutes; do not let the cooker switch to the warm setting. Use the browning (not the simmer) setting to build the sauce in step 3.

Cuban Black Beans

WHY THIS RECIPE WORKS
With their earthy flavor and touch of freshness, this recipe makes a satisfying side or simple entrée. Since they are traditionally served on the saucy side, we simply used the cooking liquid as the sauce. We browned chorizo, then sautéed onions and bell pepper in the fat. Cumin, garlic, oregano, and red pepper flakes lent an herbal, spicy undertone. After adding the broth and beans, we cooked the beans under pressure until they were almost done. After a short simmer, we stirred in the chorizo, plus oregano and cilantro. Serve over rice with lime wedges, sour cream, and hot sauce.

INGREDIENTS

2	teaspoons vegetable oil
1	pound chorizo sausage, quartered lengthwise and sliced ½-inch thick
2	onions, chopped fine
1	red bell pepper, stemmed, seeded, and cut into ½-inch pieces
1	tablespoon ground cumin
	Salt and pepper
6	garlic cloves, minced
2	tablespoons minced fresh oregano or 2 teaspoons dried
¼	teaspoon red pepper flakes
1	pound dried black beans (2 cups), picked over, rinsed, and salt-soaked (see page 18)
3	cups low-sodium chicken broth
2	bay leaves
¼	cup minced fresh cilantro

SERVES	TOTAL TIME	
6 TO 8	**ABOUT 1¼ HOURS***	
PRESSURE LEVEL	RELEASE	
HIGH	**NATURAL**	

*PLUS BEAN SOAKING TIME

25 MINUTES
UNDER PRESSURE

1. BUILD FLAVOR: Heat oil in pressure-cooker pot over medium-high heat until shimmering. Add chorizo and cook until browned, about 5 minutes; transfer to paper towel–lined plate. Add onions, bell pepper, cumin, and ¼ teaspoon salt to fat left in pot and cook over medium-high heat until vegetables are softened, about 5 minutes. Stir in garlic, 1 tablespoon oregano, and pepper flakes and cook until fragrant, about 30 seconds. Stir in beans. Stir in broth and bay leaves, scraping up any browned bits.

2. HIGH PRESSURE FOR 25 MINUTES: Lock pressure-cooker lid in place and bring to high pressure over medium-high heat. As soon as pot reaches high pressure, reduce heat to medium-low and cook for 25 minutes, adjusting heat as needed to maintain pressure.

3. NATURALLY RELEASE PRESSURE: Remove pot from heat and allow pressure to release naturally for 15 minutes. Quick release any remaining pressure, then carefully remove lid, allowing steam to escape away from you.

4. BEFORE SERVING: Discard bay leaves. Continue to simmer beans over medium heat, stirring often, until beans are tender and cooking liquid is slightly thickened, about 5 minutes. Off heat, stir in chorizo, remaining 1 tablespoon oregano, and cilantro. Season with salt and pepper to taste, and serve.

MAKING CUBAN BLACK BEANS IN A PRESSURE COOKER

Because these beans are served over rice, they are usually on the saucy side. That makes this recipe simple since the beans' cooking liquid can simply double as the sauce. We build flavor in the pot by browning chorizo, then use the rendered fat to sauté onion and bell pepper.

We found 3 cups of broth was enough liquid to ensure the beans could cook evenly, and it gave us a sauce with the right consistency at the end.

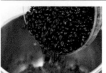
Soaking the beans overnight is key to getting beans that are cooked through evenly and hold together properly for this dish. Some beans will inevitably burst apart under pressure, but even quick-soaking methods aren't sufficient for beans prepared in a pressure cooker.

After the pressurized cooking time, we simmer the beans in the cooking liquid 5 more minutes so they can finish cooking through and the liquid can reduce. We add the chorizo at the end to ensure it stays moist, and we add more oregano plus some cilantro for a fresh, flavorful finish.

TROUBLESHOOTING

How spicy is this recipe?
These beans are fairly spicy. To make them milder, use a mild chorizo sausage and omit the red pepper flakes.

Can I make this dish vegetarian?
Yes, omit the chorizo, substitute vegetable broth for the chicken broth, and add 1 tablespoon minced chipotle in adobo sauce to the pot with the beans in step 1.

Do I need to alter the recipe for a 6-quart electric pressure cooker?
Yes, instead of relying on the cooker's built-in timer to keep track of the pressurized cooking time, use your own timer and start the countdown as soon as the pot comes to pressure. After the 25-minute cooking time, turn the cooker off immediately and let the pressure release naturally for 15 minutes; do not let the cooker switch to the warm setting. Increase the simmering time to 15 minutes in step 4, and use the browning (not the simmer) setting.

Index

A

Almonds and Cauliflower, Chickpea
Tagine with, 41
Anchovies
Puttanesca, 69
Apple(s)
Beet, and Walnut Salad, 139
Braised Red Cabbage, 142–43
and Cranberries, Pork Tenderloin
with, 86–87
Apricots, Dried, and Honey, Chickpea
Tagine with, 41
Arrabbiata, 69
Artichoke(s)
and Chickpea Tagine, 40–41
cooking in a pressure cooker, 20
with Lemon-Garlic Butter, 136–37
Asian-Style Boneless Beef Short Ribs,
108–9
Asian-Style Short Ribs with Shiitakes,
109
Asian-Style Wings, Easy, 129

B

Bacon
and Blue Cheese, Smashed Red
Potatoes with, 151
Braised Collard Greens with, 140–41
and Onions, Classic Smothered Chops
with, 84–85
Warm Potato Salad, 152–53
Barbecued Baby Back Ribs, 124–25
Barbecued Beans, 154–55
Barley
and Beef Soup, Old-Fashioned, 29

Barley *(cont.)*
cooking in a pressure cooker, 17
Basil and Sun-Dried Tomato
Polenta, 135
Bean(s)
Barbecued, 154–55
Black, and Lime Tequila Chili, 49
Black, and Sausage Chili, 49
Black, Cuban, 156–57
Black, Garden Vegetable Chili, 49
Black, Vegetarian Chili, 48–49
Boston "Baked," 155
Chicken Curry with Chickpeas and
Cauliflower, 82–83
Chickpea and Artichoke Tagine, 40–41
Chickpea Tagine with Cauliflower and
Almonds, 41
Chickpea Tagine with Dried Apricots
and Honey, 41
cooking in a pressure cooker, 18
Easy Weeknight Chili, 42–43
Easy Weeknight Chili with Moroccan
Spices and Chickpeas, 43
Fiery Texas-Style Chili con Carne, 45
15- , Soup with Sausage, 30–31
soaking, 18
Sweet and Smoky Texas-Style Chili
con Carne, 45
Texas-Style Chili con Carne, 44–45
White, and Pork Stew, Rustic
French, 36–37
Beef
and Barley Soup, Old-Fashioned, 29
Boeuf Bourguignon, 104–5
Bolognese, 62–63
Broth, 22

Beef *(cont.)*
Classic Pot Roast and Potatoes, 96–97
cooking in a pressure cooker, 19
Corned, and Cabbage, 102–3
Cuban-Style, with Onions and Bell
Peppers, 90–91
Easy Weeknight Chili, 42–43
Easy Weeknight Chili with Moroccan
Spices and Chickpeas, 43
Fiery Texas-Style Chili con Carne, 45
Italian Meatloaf, 92–93
Meatballs and Marinara, 60–61
Ragu with Warm Spices, 66–67
Short Ribs, Asian-Style,
with Shiitakes, 109
Short Ribs, Boneless,
Asian-Style, 108–9
Short Ribs, Pomegranate-
Braised, 106–7
short ribs, trimming, 67
Shredded, Soft Tacos, 89
Shredded Barbecued, 123
Sirloin, Roast with Mushroom
Sauce, 100–101
Smoky Brisket, 118–19
Stew, Hearty, 32–33
Sweet and Smoky Texas-Style Chili
con Carne, 45
Texas-Style Chili con Carne, 44–45
Tex-Mex Chili Mac, 58–59
and Vegetable Soup,
Old-Fashioned, 28–29
Weeknight Meat Sauce with
Rigatoni, 56–57
Weeknight Pot Roast and
Potatoes, 98–99
see also Veal